The Life and Times of a 'Gotcha'

James Linnane

First Published in 2011 by TAF Publishing

ISBN: 978-1-907522-38-3

A CIP Catalogue record for this book is available from
The British Library

Typesetting by James O'Sullivan

Cover Design: Karolina Smorczewska

Published with the assistance of The Author's Friend

For information about Assisted Publishing, including catalogue and
titles, visit www.TheAuthorsFriend.com

Printed and bound in Ireland by Gemini International Ltd

The Life and Times of a 'Gotcha'
Copyright James Linnane 2011

Dedicated to the three ladies in my life: Karen, Stephanie and Amber. And not forgetting our wider families and friends. Particular thanks to my sister Jane for her assistance at the eleventh hour.

Introduction

"What's a Gotcha?"

Everyone asks me, even those who should know: what's a Gotcha? A Gotcha was Dublin slang for a security guard. A word used to refer to us in many working class areas of the city where we worked and patrolled 24 hours a day, every day and every night in shifts, at that time which was mostly the 80's and 90's.

This book is based on actual events. How much is true and how much actually happened? You wouldn't believe me if I told you. Amid the boredom of a mind numbing job, sometimes emerged a madness and events which you really could not invent; you really just had to be there.

I hope you enjoy this book. I don't know if security work is still the same today. It probably is but who knows? As one book says "It was the best of times, it was the worst of times." That about sums it up.

James Linnane

Chapter 1

I started working as a security guard in Boston USA in 1985. The Boston saga of my security days was surely in a league of its own, so this is not the time in question. I returned to Dublin to live with my parents. Job hunting in Ireland then was not for the faint hearted as there was a major recession in progress at the time. Eventually after going through a few part-time jobs, I landed a job with a Dublin based security firm. I think it was May or June of 1986.

The interview went like this: I was shown into the office by the secretary. There sat two men behind desks, both between 40 and 50, one named Ron the other Aiden. We all shook hands and I sat down. Ron scrutinized my application form as though it held the secrets of eternal life. Finally a question.

"Where was your last job?"

"It says here you used to be a barman among other things...."

"Do you mind working unsociable hours..?"

"You did karate for a while ..Hmm!..."

"Were you ever arrested?..No, I see..."

I should have replied, "Not this week anyway." But of course I didn't.

"How long were you working in Boston?.. Hmm!.."

"Are you married or engaged to be?"

"You are trying to buy a house..."

"Are you ambitious to get on?..."

I thought," If I was ambitious to get on, would I be sitting here talking shit to you two wallies?"

"Have you done any safety or first aid courses?...Hmm!"

"How much money do you expect?..."

I thought, "Judging by the state of this office a lot less than I'd like to get." I wasn't wrong, but a job was a job.

"Did you ever work with guard dogs before?...No.."A slight pause, both men exchanged a glance.

"Can you start tonight?" And so it began.

They called back in the secretary and three of them set about matching me to various ragtag bits of uniform hanging on a rail in the corner. In America I was handed a pristine brand new uniform. How far the mighty had fallen!

"Have you got a blue shirt? ...Good!"

"You'll need wellies have you got them?...Good!..."

"Here's a jacket, see do these pants fit....they'll do..."

"Go home, get your blue shirt and wellies, put on your uniform, and be back outside this office to meet our supervisor at 6 o clock this evening. He will drop you to your location. Make yourself some sandwiches for tonight."

Ron offered his hand to shake and said "Welcome aboard Jim, We'll be seeing you from time to time." "Good luck" he called as I was leaving and boy would I need it.

Home I went and duly complied with all instructions. It was still afternoon and so I watched some T.V. to kill some time. I duly returned to the office at the appointed time and waited. Eventually a shifty looking fellow in a ratty hatchback Ford Fiesta pulled up in front of me, rolled down his window and in a strong Dublin accent shouted

"Are you Jim what's his name?"

"Close enough" I replied.

"Get in quick I'm in a hurry."

In I got and away we went at high speed. He drove like a getaway driver after a successful bank job. Across town we whizzed. He eyed me suspiciously all the way and there wasn't too much conversation to speak of. I could tell by the way he looked at me that he wasn't too impressed with what he saw, but I needed a job so who gave a shit what he thought? His name was Ricky. Tricky Ricky as we later christened him and Tricky he was, having dabbled on both sides of the law as I found out when I knew him better.

We arrived at a rough looking building site in Finglas where someone opened the gate. I got out and someone else got in. Tricky Ricky barked a few instructions. Zoom, zoom went the accelerator pedal and he was gone. The fellow I was on duty with was a real piece of work from Northern Ireland; hostile from the outset, ignorant, perpetually grumpy and whose conversation resembled a continuous growl. I had and have previously worked with many people from Northern Ireland and I have always liked them well enough, but this guy had very few, if any, redeeming features or if he did he kept them well hidden. Yes indeed a dyed in the wool dickhead; awkward to work with, unfriendly, menacing and generally a pain in the arse. The twelve-hour night shift seemed long indeed, would morning never come? For all intents and purposes I would say he was an out and out nutter. Mind you, sometime later he said he thought the same about me – I suspect we were both right. Though possibly I may have hammed it up a bit in a kind of defensive mode, sort of like saying , "Don't fuck with me I'm a headcase too."

From time to time he would read me fiery passages from "An Phoblacht" *(a Republican newspaper)*. At that time the troubles were in full swing and all we in the south of Ireland understood of what was going on north of the border was what we were told by the media, which I am sure was selective enough in what we were allowed to know. At that time most of us were too scared to go across the border, let alone know what was really going on there, save what we were told. This guy ranting on about this stuff was making me nervous indeed. This, after the "Hi! Have a nice Day" attitude of Boston. The funny thing was I later befriended another officer who was involved with Sinn Fein (An illegal organization at that time). My friend told me this fellow was the biggest bull-shitter of all time; had no actual involvement in anything, other than talking copious quantities of crap. I have always felt sorry for the people in the North who had to endure the troubles and listening to this guy fairly turned my stomach with, his particular view point. My friend said that he loaned him the paper but that he couldn't stand him either.

But the crowning glory of the site, aside from the squalor, aside from the derelict state of the place, aside from the local youths pelting us with stones, trying to steal from the site, to set fire to the guard dogs or to cause havoc in one way or another, was a particular schizophrenic guard dog named Roddy. An evil looking Alsatian with a half mad gleam in his eye, who could turn on you for no reason at all. He was an oldish dog, with a dark coloured coat. His favourite pastime was lying on the floor, perpetually licking his gross looking penis, which seemed to grow to about a foot long and about an inch and a half in diameter. His frantic licking would climax when he would ejaculate into his own mouth and gobble it down with gusto. Usually I had to have some air after this performance, if the dog would let me out the door. My Northern friend seemed to enjoy all this immensely. I even suspect he envied the dog's ability a bit. At one stage while I was having a sandwich and cup of tea, the dog seized my foot and began to shake it, growling viciously. My Northern friend dragged him off me. He seemed to understand the dog and his psychology.

He explained "You looked into the dog's eyes while eating your sandwich and did not offer him any." By this I gathered he was hungry as well as psychopathic. "Crazy fucking Nordy, crazy fucking dog" I thought, "so this is hell then."

I made a note of this piece of information for future reference. That dog didn't like you standing behind him; didn't and often wouldn't go through doorways, for love, threats or bribes and was prone to violent mood swings. Sometimes you were the enemy. Always keep a baton handy in case of attack. He could totally ignore an intruder and suddenly turn on his handler for no reason. You just never knew what to expect. He didn't like sharing the security hut, hated being locked in sheds and generally scared the shit out of me. The general treatment of guard dogs was appalling and I suppose that explained some of their dispositions and ill will towards humanity as a whole. They were starved, abused, left out in the rain, and belted with sweeping brushes, had missiles hurled at them from outside the fence and sundry other miseries to contend with. We were called 'Gotchas' locally.

As time went on I met many other officers; nearly all seemed to be immediate candidates for a mental home, if not prison. A good many already had convictions. I found out that a few had served short sentences. I began to suspect this was no superior working class establishment. I spent many the miserable night in the company of these strange life forms and bemoaned the fact that I had ever left America and my then, sweetheart. It was the early days of security when the security guards were more likely to be thieves than the thieves themselves. "Bad old days" might be putting it mildly.

As autumn drew near the rain turned the whole site into a quagmire of foot deep muck. We trudged around in Wellingtons and work boots, cursing life in general. I suspect some of my criminal friends wished they were back behind bars.

Elsewhere, one security guard freshly recruited, was left overnight to mind a public house with a guard dog for company. They found him in the morning up on a snooker table, keeping the guard dog at bay with one of the cues. The guard dog didn't like him much. On the phones we rang everywhere we could; from New York to Turkey, to Norway, to anywhere. Some of the boys when they got bored would go through the phone book, pick a number, any number, leaving fucked up messages on answering machines, or just wake people up and insult them. Sometimes, picking on the same person all night, ringing every few hours. Someone filled my wellies with concrete on my day off and it set inside them. I somehow managed to bash it out of them. The building company got a phone bill for £10,000, a fortune at that time, and everyone blamed everyone else. The security firm threatened hell fire and brimstone on us all. Someone pointed the finger at me and I was almost sacked. Calls were not traceable at that time and proving anything was nigh impossible. Also, of course, the few calls I made, while not exactly cheap, sure didn't come to £10,000.

Some of us spent the night trying to protect what was on site, others spent it loading up the trunk of their car with anything they fancied. One fellow even tried to rob a cash box of its contents, but he could not force it open with the knife he had. The guard dogs were kept in a couple of sheds in the interim period, between when the security guard went home, the workers arrived and the dog van collected the dog. The workers might have had tools or clothes in these sheds and invariably they would forget about the guard dogs and march into the wrong shed, the guard dog was trained for one thing and it did it. Some got bitten, some were quick enough to escape. It was a bit like Russian roulette and always someone picked the wrong shed. I remember one ex-army fellow called Ryan, who ate what he called health food instead of sandwiches, like the rest of us. It consisted of nuts, dried fruit and other queer looking stuff, washed down with copious quantities of water. When he farted in the hut it was time to run for cover, a bit like Hiroshima revisited. I tried to enlighten him about the dogs. He put on a mean looking face and produced a big sheath knife and said, "Ya see dat, if one dem fuckers comes near me I'll cut his bleedin' throat."

"Fair enough," said I and left it at that.

About a week later I was talking to one of the lads who told me our Nordy screwball had incorrectly handed Ryan a dog after a patrol. The dog took offence and immediately sunk his teeth into Ryan's arm. Our intrepid knife fighter screamed like a baby, dropped the lead and ran for his life. The dog overtook him, knocked him to the ground, sunk his teeth into his back and began to savage him. Screwball dragged him off just in time by the collar (the dog I mean).

After he got out of hospital he sued the building site; the dog owner of course; the security firm and anyone else he could think of. At least it was one battle he won. Last I heard of him was that he took the money and went to Spain to try to become an artist, a pacifist at heart after all. The poor doggy was put down. I quite liked that particular one, but there you go.

Dogs generally like people and it is not a natural phenomenon for them to be aggressive towards people, normally speaking, so they have to be "trained" to attack. This essentially amounts to tormenting them, abusing them, hitting and such.

I was told that in some part of Germany where they used to train Dobermans as attack dogs, they would use techniques such as sealing them in a metal barrel and beating the barrel until the dog was half insane: dogs have very sensitive hearing. They would torment and torture them in various ways until they became vicious. They did such a good job, that if the dog ever saw the fellow again who had trained him, he would try to kill him. So, as you can well imagine, there weren't too many tearful annual reunions between dog and trainer. It was best for the trainer that they did not meet again.

I'm sure Irish trainers weren't too kindly either. As I said "poor doggy they just couldn't win."

Chapter 2

On one of the other sites another guard got sacked. When on duty at a fast food outlet he developed a penchant for chasing girls into the ladies' toilet. It got so bad, they were scared to go for a wee. Yet another, an ex-Irish Navy man came onto the premises blind drunk, as was his wont, on his day off. He spotted some fellow he didn't like, he started an argument with him and his girlfriend and duly punched both of them. A free for all broke out and Vinny wound up on the floor with a number of people on top of him, kicking and punching him. The officer on duty got a baton from behind the counter and promptly waded in trying to save Vinny. A number of people were injured including a woman. The supervisor was called by radio. He arrived just as the police arrived and for a while it was a tossup as to who got locked up: the security guards or the customers. In the end the police were so confused everyone was let go and Vinny wobbled his way back to the pub, happy as you like. Of course he got chucked out in the end, but surprisingly not for some time. He told a fellow working in the cash box in a car park while on duty "No, I don't drink at all."

The cash box man Fran had a major drink problem himself and knew the truth immediately. I suppose the shaky hands gave it away. Anyhow, a short while later, Fran was watching the C.C.T.V. and observed good old Vinny at the other end of the car park looking furtively around him before whipping out a hip flask and downing half the contents. Probably a health supplement, don't you think? Anyway, when he came back from his hard patrol he was in much better form, if not a bit wobbly and the fumes would curl your hair. After a while we all became aware his hip flask was a permanent fixture with him. I don't think he could actually function without it.

The car parks were undoubtedly a saga in themselves. The

attendants, i.e. the people who took the cash from the drivers on the way out, were of even worse calibre than we were, (which was pretty bad). Mostly from rough Dublin backgrounds, their one thing in common being an extreme fondness for alcohol. Their lives were one big drinking binge. They would spend a few hours in the car parks until the bosses went home and then grab some money from the till proceeding directly to the pub. Sometimes they would take turns on duty in the cash box while the other was on the beer. However, if the one on pub duty didn't come back when he said he would, the strain would become too much for the poor fellow left behind and he would also go to the pub to seek solace with his friends, leaving the unfortunate security guard on duty to fend for himself. Consequently, we all became very familiar with the use of said tills. Some, unfortunately, became a bit too familiar and occasionally helped themselves to a little gratuity for their trouble. One of our number remarked to an attendant, "I'm going to case this joint for me mates to rob," or words to that effect. A robbery happened fairly soon afterwards. One of the thieves was apprehended and surprise, surprise, he lived around the corner from our friend. I think he was gradually eased out as opposed to outright sacked, as nothing was proven. South Dublin I think it was, he lived.

Of course it is not true to say that we were all lunatics, up to every kind of mischief. I give prominence to the more spectacular events, which occurred, simply because they were spectacular. I mean the core of the job was mundane, tedious routine: patrolling buildings, yards, warehouses, locking and unlocking doors and gates, clocking keys in a time clock as we patrolled, at the relevant key points, asking people to move cars, calling the police when something serious occurred, checking temperature gauges in factories, setting alarms, responding to alarms, making sure electric pumps were working and switched on and so on. In the daytime we might have to check dockets from lorry drivers going out gates, to ensure that their loads corresponded with what it said on paper, before they were allowed to leave the premises. We raised or lowered barriers , accordingly, to let people in or out etc.

The bosses and directors of these places were usually around during the daytime and occasionally one would leave his warm, comfy office and come out in the cold to give us shit about something or other, whether, merely perceived or actual: i.e. "Why was that barrier up, it should be kept down at all times...?" Or vice versa.

"Why were you not wearing a tie?"

"Why did you let that car park there?"

"Who was that scruffy fellow and why did you let him get by you?"

"Where's your site helmet?"

"Why were you eating a sandwich while talking to a customer?"And on and on and on...

At night, however, you were mostly left alone, saving a visit from the mobile supervisor, who had to drive around all night, checking on various premises and on us. Night time was a long, lonely, dreary vigil, punctuated by hourly patrols, around yards or factories, clocking keys or checking those gauges mentioned earlier. If it was a dangerous location you were sometimes given a guard dog. Some locations had a more sinister aura at night, simply put, they were scary as hell in the dark. I remember one such location where some of the daytime workers, as a joke, had dressed up a mannequin and left it in the canteen. At night, as I was patrolling I invariably forgot it was there and would see the silhouette of someone looking out at me in the dark and almost wet my pants. Still, at night you were mostly left alone and there was indeed always the possibility of sneaking in forty winks, somewhere along the way. Mainly, the point that I am making here, is that there were many officers who took the job seriously, worked at it diligently, showed up on time, impeccably dressed, uniform ironed and clean, themselves, well groomed and clean shaven. Further, they would put in an effort on every shift as if it were their first, as opposed to others, who were normally slovenly dressed, unshaven, half sober and could generally care less if the whole place they were guarding, burned down around their ears. They did as little as possible, slept most of their nightshifts, where possible, stole what wasn't nailed down and mostly had no interest in the job, except when it came to collecting their wages. Me?...Well I was somewhere in the middle, between the two species. Though I have to say, in my own defence, mostly I was an honest and relatively diligent soul. In other words, I showed up for duty, put in some semblance of a work shift, filled in my report sheet and went happily home.

A report sheet contained your name; the name of the contract you were on; the time you came on duty; the time you went home; who replaced you and when he arrived; when and if, you let anyone in or out, including your supervisor; anything unusual that happened while you were on duty, and you also had to mark it in, every time you did a patrol. Usually it went like this:

"Time 1900 hours. Patrolled premises, checked boundary fence: all in order. Nothing to report."

Riveting stuff, wasn't it? Can't you just feel the tension, like a coiled spring? Me neither. Well anyhow I got in plenty of reading and I even managed to write a bit, including, what were the humble beginnings of this book, such as it is or was or would be.

I remember talking to my friend Stevie on the phone one night discussing some of the mad events which took place over the years and I remarked "I would love to write a book about it all someday." He replied "Sure who'd believe it Jimmy, it's all too crazy."

"I suppose you're right Stevie" I said "but wouldn't it be some laugh?"

"It sure would, let me know I'll buy a copy," he joked.

"That I will" I said.

That night we were both on duty in different parts of Dublin and I never really dreamed I would get around to writing this properly. Still it seems I did all the same and if it transpires the book isn't that entertaining to read, it is more a testament to my inadequacies as a writer than the material, because even now, years later, so many of these events still make me laugh out loud. Now I am not saying that there was no embellishment, maybe a bit of jazzing up here and there, maybe an occasional bit of fiction thrown in now and again, and some of the stories had to be toned down or even omitted for one reason or another but this story is certainly based on fact. All names except my own and I do mention my daughter towards the end, are absolutely fiction. So here's hoping I have told my tale well.

Chapter 3

Anyhow, the party went on in the car parks, for the attendants. One night I was on duty as one fellow nipped back and forth to the pub and then did not return at all until everyone was gone and I had locked up. He returned literally stinking drunk, having drunk so much he actually shit his pants and was unaware of it. The smell was unbearable. It was a freezing night, but, cold as it was, I had to get outside the box for air when he arrived.

"Stan' in the box ou' the cold," he said considerately. "It's fuckin' freezing."

"I'm not cold," said I, shivering away outside. He tried to do the cash but couldn't.

"C'm in," he said grabbing my arm. "Coun' tha'," pointing to the cash.

The smell persisted and now he had sat on the seat I had to sit on. "Nothing for it," I thought. So, trying hard not to be sick I sat in the chair. I had been a barman and a manager once, so doing the cash was not so hard in itself, but, boy that smell! He stood with his arse close to my nose while I struggled with my figures. So I finished the cash and wrote down my totals on his sheet. I checked them twice. He tried to focus on the sheet but could not.

"Sis' wrong," so saying he grabbed the sheet, crumpled it up and threw it in the bin. "Check a' again and get dah fuckin' ting' rih."

I was very tired, it had been a long day. "Paddy," I said "It is right."

"No way Jimmy, its fuckin' wrong, do a' again."

Then like an adult with an idiot child he spoke nicely to me, beseeching me to show a bit of reason. I counted it again and again. I think in the end he said something like, "Ah fuck a', it'll have to do." He retrieved the crumpled up sheet from the bin and jammed the lot down the chute into the night safe. Then, shitty trousers and all, he got into his car and drove off home, somehow. The amount of fiddling of cash that took place in those car parks should have been in the Guinness Book of Records. One fellow was caught on his knees in an outdoor car park adjusting the time clock with a screwdriver. This being part of a complicated process of fiddling the till. I think he was sacked. The methods of bypassing the so-called 'infallible' till were ingenious: from making their own master key, to electrically bypassing the circuit to lift the barrier, without involving the till.

In other words, to take the money without the till knowing. It was explained to me once by one of the attendants, twice. I'm still not sure if I understood the entire process, even now, so I won't try to explain it to you.

Now and again a row would break out down in some pub where they were drinking and all hell would break loose and they would all come back happier than usual. On one occasion an argument broke out between an attendant and a customer. I think the man realised he had been overcharged and when he complained the attendant called him a "Gobshite college yuppie." The customer foolishly challenged him to a fight saying "If you were a man you'd come out of that box and fight me."

"Fair enough," said Fergus, tucking something up his sleeve as he left the box. The customer duly put up his fists and Fergus then produced the hammer from up his sleeve and flattened him with one swipe. When the customer could speak and said that was not exactly his understanding of a fair fight, Fergus replied, "Oh, I must've gone to a different school than you."

Chapter 4

The General Manager of the car parks had an exciting time, trying hard to maintain control. Confrontations were always good for a few laughs, as the workers total disregard for him was comical to behold.

On one occasion he visited an outside car park only to find one of the attendants was missing. His workmates made various excuses for him "He's gone for change," and so on. He had accepted this and was about to leave when the workers spotted Jacky weaving his way towards them, manfully working along the wall. He did not spot the G.M. or the little signals from his pals. He finally made it to the box where the G.M. confronted him.

"Now then Jacky, I think you have a drink or two taken."

Jacky was incredulous, aghast at what he saw as the man's idiotic understatement, "A drink or two?" he replied, "What do you mean? Sure I'm fuckin' twisted."

On another occasion in a fit of rage the G.M. said to one of the men, "I want to see you in the office first thing Monday morning."

Came the reply; "Sure, I'd be no good in the office Mr. Boyle, you'd be better off leaving me here in the car park, that's what I'm good at."

Elsewhere in a coal yard the Operations Manager got sick of seeing a certain security guard asleep in a nice comfortable chair at the main gate hut. So one evening after work he took the chair out, poured petrol over it and set it on fire. Meanwhile we were feeling ridiculous wandering around the coal yard perimeter in all kinds of weather. The thieves had a lookout system to signal each other as to our whereabouts so that while we were on the opposite side of the yard they got busy going in through holes in the fence to steal coal. There was a large horse belonging to one of the thieves, used to carry stolen coal, who would stay in one spot no matter how I tried to chase him away, while the owner hid in the bushes nearby, waiting for me to go. Many of the thieves were ex-employees whose friends, still working inside, would use their mechanical shovels to shove coal to the edge of the fence for their pals to steal; a late redundancy package, I suppose.

In a large house where we did security in a certain part of Coolock, which is in North Dublin, a security guard got a bit careless with two guard dogs kept in the house; one was to be collected. Guard dogs, it should be said, are trained to attack and generally hate the sight of each other. Anyhow, Mick was coming down the stairs with a guard dog trotting in front of him. The door of the room downstairs had not been locked properly. Lo and behold, open it swung. The dog inside saw the one outside and, hey presto, the charge of the light brigade was nothing compared to the melee that ensued. Unfortunately, both dogs were unleashed and there was no way to stop them. In an effort to seize one of them Mick lost his balance, tripped over his moped, left in the hallway, and crashed down in a heap with the moped on top of him, the two dogs still fighting beside him. The dogs were trying their best to kill each other. In his desperation Mick took off his shoes and threw them at the dogs with absolutely no effect. He did somehow manage to separate them, I think there was a chair involved and got them back into separate rooms. He was still shaking when I arrived on duty, shortly afterwards.

One night as shifts ended, we were all being collected by the supervisor to bring us home in the little Ford fiesta van. We were all squeezing in any way we could. It was late; all the buses were off duty so it was the only way for to get home, if we had no car, which most of us didn't.

We were in Dublin city centre. Two lads squeezed into the front seat. There were no seats in the back and three or four lads were stretched out lengthwise head to toe i.e. lying with their feet in the other man's face and vice versa. There were no windows in the back to open. Unfortunately Colin, a relatively new recruit was head to toe with Fintan. Fintan it should be said, had a reputation for many things, but personal hygiene was not one of them and he was one of the very few men that I have met in my life whose smelly socks could stifle you without him taking off his shoes and I mean they stank. I actually think that he never changed them, or at least not more than once a year. The smell was not like ordinary sweaty socks, rather they had an aura of something that had died and was in an advanced state of decay. So it was that we were not far down the road when Colin began to fairly shout, "Stop the van let me out, let me out."

While we believed he did suffer a bit from claustrophobia I'd say myself it was the socks that did the trick."What's wrong Colin" enquired the driver.

"I said stop the fuckin' van and let me out, I want to walk."

"But Colin you live miles away."

Now Colin became quite shrill. "I said let me out ya' bastard I want to walk." This last he almost screamed and was getting more hysterical by the second. Nicky pulled over and unlocked the rear door to let him out. Colin with bulging eyes almost fell out onto the road. At this stage he was hyperventilating and sweating profusely.

"Are ya alright Colin?"

"I'm grand."

"Are ya sure you're alright?"

"I'm fuckin' grand I said."

The normally mild mannered Colin had lost it, assuming he had it in the first place.

"Are ya sure ya want to walk home at this hour of the night?"

"Yeah, yeah I'm grand, sorry an' all, I'll be grand thanks."

"Fair enough goodnight so."

"Night Nicky thanks."

And so we left him in the middle of Dublin, in the dead of night, with a long walk home.

As we drove away Fintan shifted his position in the back, giving us all a good noseful of his feet and said "Janey mac, I wonder wha' came over poor oul' Colin; must be them bleedin' long night shifts."

None of us answered him, we were all holding our breath.

Chapter 5

Across from the house was a hotel which was also owned by those who owned the house and so, on occasion, we filled in for the recently employed night porter, who knew as much about security as I knew about shark fishing. In other words, not a lot. He saw us using guard dogs, so he wanted one too. He asked the hotel and, to my amazement, they gave him one, with no instructions or training. They hired it from the same company as we did. Within about a month there was hardly a member of staff who had not been bitten or attacked by the animal due to careless handling of an otherwise excellent guard dog.

Each night the dog would be placed in a different hotel room where he would promptly shit for want of being brought outside for a walk. As the same room was not used consecutively, the staff would never know which room he was in. Back to the old Russian Roulette scenario. Of course, someone almost always went into the wrong room, with obvious consequences. If this was not bad enough, old Buck Rodgers, as we called him, would let the dog out unleashed, after closing time, to trot around as he pleased and of course when the bow-wow saw a member of staff, or a customer leaving the premises late, his training kicked in. The really fast runners usually got away, well, sometimes. Even when waitresses or staff members did get bitten, the intrepid Buck Rodgers did not seem remotely troubled. When I asked him about this, came the reply, "Ah, sure they'll get used to him."

The dog would trot in behind the bar where the poor bar staff were cleaning up; it had a similar effect to throwing a hand grenade into a bunker, with people bailing out on all sides, over the counter and such.

One night a row broke out involving two big male 'travellers' and the doorman. The doorman Desy was manfully struggling with the culprits. "Get the dog, get the dog!" he shouted at Buck, who was delighted to comply. He came back into the crowded bar with the dog on a leash, seeing all these "intruders" the doggie went into overdrive. People knocked over tables, spilled drinks, stood on top of each other trying to get out of the way. Rex lunged at everyone, teeth snapping. People dived under tables and climbed on seats to get to safety. When Buck and Rex got to the fracas one of the travellers shouted,

"Keep that fucking dog away from me or I'll kill 'um," and so saying proceeded to kick the already half crazed dog, who was held in such a way by Buck as to be within range of kicks, but unable to retaliate. Seeing this, Buck lost it, "Right you bastard, that's it."

And to the amazement of all, unleashed the, by now insane, animal who went hurtling into the affray and promptly sunk his teeth into the doorman's groin. The dog had to be retrieved and locked up again. The police arrived, a number of people were injured, one of the travellers also. An ambulance came. One fellow was taken away by police, another put in an ambulance. As soon as the police had gone and the ambulance was moving off, the doors of the ambulance were kicked open and the traveller inside jumped out and ran off down the road. Later on I had the misfortune to be sitting at the bar when the doorman insisted on pulling down his trousers to show us how close he had come to losing his balls. All he had underneath was a plastic groin protector, which doubtless saved him, no underwear and a set of great big teeth marks on the inside of his thigh. Close indeed. If I had not been there that night I probably wouldn't believe it either, but I was. The sight of the doorman's tackle, I could certainly have done without. The saga of Buck Rodgers was not over yet. The hotel had been prone to frequent robberies so Buck got nervous and wanted one of our radios so we could check on him if he got in trouble and come over from the house.

One night I was on duty in the house. I checked in with Buck every couple of hours. At closing time when everyone was gone I usually went over for a chat. This night he sounded a bit strange, "Don't come over yet, the chef is doing a stock take in the kitchen."

I looked at my watch: 3:00am. A stock take, well, well. I went over and looked for signs of something not right. No broken windows, no look outs, no strange cars, all was locked up, so I could not get in. At 5:00am I tried the radio again. No reply. So I again went over, looked in all the windows and finally I knocked and shouted until he appeared. His hair was standing on end and he smelled strongly of drink when he grudgingly let me in. I asked him was something wrong, "Come on, I'll show ya."

He brought me to a room where I peered through the slightly open door to see the tousled head of a half naked woman lying on a bed. He told me she was a "dirty bitch" and she was "mad for it" and he had been "givin' her one." He asked me if I'd like to give her one too.

"With the lights off she'll never know the difference. She'll think it's me. She wouldn't mind anyway, she's a dirty bitch, she loves it."

I declined the offer even though times were hard, but vision's of her waking up screaming, dampened any ideas I might have had. He then began to worry about having contracted V.D. or A.I.D.S. and then asked me if I thought whiskey would kill germs. Not thinking, I said it probably would. When I walked into the bar a few minutes later there stood Buck with his trousers around his ankles, baptizing his penis, while holding it with one hand and dousing it liberally with a large bottle of Irish whiskey.

Chapter 6

Another guard was caught, after loading up a friend's lorry with a great deal of the contents of a roofing supplies yard, just as he was directing him out the gate at about 5:00am. Neighbours to the factory heard all the commotion at that strange hour and notified the police. As the lorry pulled out the special branch swooped in on it in unmarked cars. Seeing this, the security man ran in and locked himself in the toilet, to be coaxed out later on and sacked.

Back on the building site in Finglas, the Foreman, who was hated by one and all, was tormenting a guard dog tied to a pole. The dog's lunges snapped the lead. I have never seen a foreman put on such a turn of speed in my life. Our disappointment was palpable when he managed to get to his car just ahead of the dog. Mind you, his face was so pale and his eyes bulging and frightened, it helped to console us a little anyhow. We then rounded up the dog to avoid harming any other workers.

Sometimes, on the two way radio, one heard some entertaining moments. At one stage a new guard was placed in a derelict building near Baggot Street in South Dublin. Here, let me say that the isolation of security work and indeed, many of the locations are not for the faint hearted. Right, well anyway, I think he saw a couple of rats or something. The first we heard was him contacting the mobile supervisor.

"Come in, mobile, come in."

"Mobile here, go ahead."

"Get me out of here quick," he wailed.

"What's wrong?"

"Get me out of here; I want to go home to me mammy. I don't want to be here."

"What's wrong? What happened?"

At this stage he began to blubber and became fairly incoherent. It was clear he had totally lost it. The Supervisor had to go and collect him and bring him home. He blubbered and babbled all the way home. Next day he dropped his uniform to the office and said,

"Mammy said I'm not to work for you anymore. Goodbye."

Never to be seen again, amen. Another poor fellow, a bit simple, again, this was all on air, locked himself in a room in an office block he was guarding,

"Mobile, mobile, I'm locked in. What'll I do?"

"Where are you?"

"I'm locked in, help me!"

"What floor are you on?"

"I don't know, get me out."

"I'm on my way, I'm across town."

"Hurry, in the name of God."

Twenty minutes later.

"I'm not far from you now David."

"Come in mobile," sounding rather coy.

"Go ahead."

"I'm alright now. It's okay."

"What happened?"

"I was just pushing the door the wrong way. It wasn't locked at all. I was pushing and it said 'pull' on the door. Sorry."

"David, you're a bloody half wit, don't call me again tonight you bloody moron."

"Okay mobile" (subdued voice). He didn't last too long either.

On a more serious note, we also had a guard on said building site in Finglas, before my arrival, who had stolen all the lead off the roof of the factory being renovated. Ditto went all copper piping and wiring, etc. and was making great money selling it for scrap. Of course if anyone commented, he would have blamed it on the local ruffians.

Before he was eventually sacked he had molested a number of young children, forcing a young local boy to masturbate him in a corner of the factory at knife point. He also raped a 12 year old girl in a loft in the factory and left the poor girl pregnant. Among his final deeds after being sacked were to come back to the factory with his gang, kick the shit out of the new guards and finally throw them out of an upper window, hospitalizing both. He and his buddies later came across a young couple necking in a car. They dragged both out and beat the crap out of the boy and locked him in the trunk. They then turned their attention on the girl. They raped her, sodomised her, burned her with cigarette butts. Each had their turn and finally they rammed broken bottles up her private parts, kicking them into her. Apparently the girl survived. He got life in prison for this. I'm inclined to think it wasn't enough. Someone told me that the reason he had got away with his deeds for so long was that he was a police informant and so they left him alone. I hope the information he gave them was worth it, though somehow I doubt it very much.

Chapter 7

Back to the lighter side, and the madness still went on in most other security firms as well as ours. At one stage a firm had men working along the docks to mind new cars being shipped in. The keys were in the ignition for moving them. At first, the guards just drove them around a bit. That was okay.

One night a race developed and they all went slightly berserk. One fellow ploughed into a row of nice shiny new cars and another wound up in the water. The guards were not too badly injured, but rather than face the wrath of their superiors, they all ran away, never to be seen again and that was how the workers found it next day. Crashed cars all over the place and one missing car was eventually found under water.

Another event on a building site full of lorries and machinery, was, when an experienced officer sent out a new recruit to patrol while he was having a break. It had been some time since the young man had gone out and there was no sign of him. It was pitch dark. The older man was about to go and check on him, when he saw one of the forty foot lorries hurtling towards him all lights on! In a panic, he ran out to close the main gate to stop the lorry getting out. Then he ran back to the hut, to radio for help. Just as he had the radio in one hand and was dialling the police on the phone with the other, the lorry sped by and the driver blew his horn and waved. The older man stared in disbelief as he recognised the driver, the new recruit. He circled the site and hurtled by again with the window down. The older guard shouted, "What the fuck are you doing?"

"Ah, sure, I'm just using the big torch," came the reply.

Yet another event in the same firm where a new recruit was left on a spooky sort of site which was prone to break-ins. In the early part of the night he radioed for help and said he'd been attacked by a gang. It did happen sometimes, so the supervisor arrived and the police were called. The guard was there covered in muck and looking shaky. The hut was a mess with everything broken or upended. He gave vague descriptions to the Gardaí, who subsequently left. He told the supervisor he was very badly shaken and couldn't finish the shift.

So a replacement was found and he was brought home. The next morning the replacement (a friend of mine) was doing his rounds when he struck up a conversation with the guard next door, in a large factory, who was also doing his final patrol. During the conversation the other fellow kept examining my friend's uniform which was clean and ironed. As he was about to go he turned to my friend and said, "Ya know it's terrible the way your eyes can play tricks on you in the dark."

"How do ya mean?"

"Well, last night I could have sworn I saw you rollin' around in muck on your own. I thought you'd gone a bit mad."

My friend of course realised his fellow officer must have really wanted the night off, badly.

Another facet was still the persistent ill-treatment of the unfortunate, often hopelessly loyal and fearless dogs, by the firms who owned them. Many in later years were brought to court because of this, some were closed down. At Christmas, for instance, a certain amount of food would be left for the dog, about 2 days worth. The dog owner would sod off for about 2 weeks, during which time the big dogs would become ravenously hungry for the remaining time. One poor guard when he could no longer control the hungry dog and was getting a bit scared of it. He unleashed it. It immediately galloped off to the fields where it found and killed two sheep and ate half of one of them.

One of our supervisors was a bit of a dickhead who did not have much hair and an attitude like Adolph Hitler. So, when possible, my friend and I would warn each other when he left us, to say he was on his way, by landline of course, no mobiles then. Why Stevie delayed so long to ring me, I don't know, but by the time he did, Conway had arrived. As he entered, the phone rang. He picked it up before I could and did not speak. I distinctly heard Stevie say,

"That fat, little, baldy fuck is on his way round to you now Jimmy."

"Oh shit," I thought.

The tirade he unleashed on poor Stevie was a fright to behold. Somewhere along the line it must have occurred to Stevie that he was 6' foot 1" and the Supervisor giving him abuse was a little runt.

"Go and fuck yourself you arrogant little prick. If I see you again tonight I'll put my fist through ya."

He hung up. I knew Stevie meant it. Conway started to rant at how he'd report Stevie and get him sacked and he warned me to watch myself too. Obviously he was hitting all the right buttons with me too, because Stevie was my friend for many years.

So I said "I'm with this company a long time and you're six months here, so here it is, if you report Stevie I'll ring every man in this outfit and get them all to complain about you to head office and so will I. If needs be, I'll organise a walk out until they sack you. See if I don't. So like Stevie said, go fuck yourself."

I don't know if he did go and fuck himself but, as far as I know, he didn't report him. We worked together for some years after that, me and Stevie. Conway lasted another four months, after that and he quit. During his remaining time he treaded a bit more carefully around me and Stevie and almost apologised to Stevie. I don't really know if I could have got him fired, but I had intended to try my best. Nobody was too sad when he left. The hours were long and the job hard enough without Conway giving us crap.

Chapter 8

There was a famous tennis tournament on, sometime later. Myself and another, an ex-army fellow, were on duty. He had a chronic drink problem. He had been sacked previously for showing up for duty drunk, crashing into the gate in front of the hut, he fell out of the car and staggered up to the hut for duty, where the contracts manager was standing with his mouth open in shock. He tore a strip off him and sent him home. His son also worked for the firm and both pleaded with the boss to give him another chance. This he did. At the end of the tournament there was a celebration night. As it transpired Barney and I were on duty together. There was a marquee outside the tennis clubhouse. He was on duty in the car park and I in the club house. When I arrived and met him, I smelled the fumes, I knew he had been drinking. I liked old Barney for all his faults, he'd done me no harm and I didn't want to see him sacked for good. I said "Barney, for God's sake, don't say you have drink on you. This is your last chance. If you're caught again you're gone. No problem Jim."

"I'll tell you, I ran into the old army major I used to know and he "forced me" to go up to the club house and have a drink with him and sure, you know, I had to be sociable, so I just had 3 treble brandies and a pint of beer."

"Holy shit," I thought "if I drank that I'd be on the floor."

Out loud I said "Barney, no more booze please. I can only cover for you so much."

"Don't worry Jim. I'm as good as gold. No more for me tonight."

"Good man." The night wore on and most people left. I radioed him and we met at the club house door. He said there was four guys gang banging two girls in the corner of the beer tent, so he left them to it. Eventually, they too left and I asked Barney if he wanted a cup of tea.

"No, no, Jim, I'm grand."

I did my radio checks every couple of hours but, I noticed his voice getting just a bit slurred. 4:00am – no reply. 6:00am – no reply. Time to have a look see. The supervisor arrived as I was going out. Unlike our other supervisor, Benny from Belfast was a decent guy, but I feared the worst for Barney. He came in, had a cup of tea, signed my sheet and then enquired about Barney. He radioed him to come on up. No reply. So down we went, down to the tent. There, asleep on a trestle table, wrapped in a tablecloth, surrounded by half drunk pints and fully drunk ones of every type of beer in the tent, lay Barney. Benny shook him. The comatose Barney opened his bleary eyes, muttered something incoherent and lay down again. He had been a barman in the army, so like me, he knew how to retap kegs and turn on gas to the kegs which had been switched off when staff left and this he had done. He drank till he could drink no more and then passed out. We lifted him up and helped him up to the club house.

"I'm awright, I'm awright."

We let him go and he wobbled all over the place, so Benny said, and rightly,

"If they see him we'll all be run out of it."

He meant the club workers. So he told him to leave his car and dropped him to a bus stop. He came back to replace him, himself. Twenty minutes later Benny and I were talking. Benny's back was to the window and over his shoulder I could see a crouching figure slinking along behind the hedge. A minute later out drove Barney at high speed. That was the last time I saw poor old Barney. Of course this time he was sacked for good. Me and Benny cleared up some of the glasses and I put the kegs back the way they had been. End of story. Bye, bye Barney.

Yet another new guy started with us. I did not have much conversation with him. He was late thirties, going slightly bald, medium build, a bit surly and distant."I think he's a bit odd meself," pronounced a fellow officer.

Even when I was talking to him I always perceived him to be receiving on a different channel to the one I was actually broadcasting on. I believe the term 'on another planet' might well apply in this case. Anyhow, for what it's worth his name was J.J. Now in fairness if being a bit crazy precluded one from being a security guard, I feel certain this criteria would have dispensed with everyone in the firm including the bosses and especially me. So the craziness was not the problem, a bit like deodorant, it was really just the brand he was using that didn't suit. I suppose there are degrees: you know, a bit eccentric, slightly crazy, a bit mad, a total fruitcake, an out and out nutter and so on. Perhaps we really should have developed some kind of points system, so much for howling at the moon, so much for molesting the guard dogs, so much for biting people, exposing yourself in public, rooting in rubbish bins for food, chasing cars and so on. Well I confess I never did work this one out fully and I must immediately point out that to my knowledge nobody did any of the aforementioned things, well, not exactly.

To continue, we were doing night security in a large well known hospital in Dublin city, mostly doing night porter type stuff, keeping an eye on who went in and out or got access to the wards, lending a hand when some inebriated or drug-crazed headcase would lose the plot in casualty and turn a bit psycho, locking and unlocking doors for the nurses and other staff and so on.

We had a man at each end of the hospital and although we had radio contact we usually did not meet until we were going home in the morning. J.J. was on duty at the hospital quite a bit. A while after he started, one of the nurses approached me and said,

"That J.J. makes me a bit nervous, he's always hanging around our changing rooms and our lockers. Is he a bit weird or something?"

I said I did not know the guy very well or very long.

"Why do you think he's weird anyway?"

"I went to the locker room the other night to change and there he was stretched out on a bench holding a pair of women's underwear to his nose with his other hand down his trousers and him gruntin' and moanin' out of him. I got the fright of my life..... bloody pervert.....he was so busy he didn't even notice me."

It was extremely hard for me to keep a straight face.

"So what did you do?"

"I went out and slammed the door real loud going out. I waited in the room across the hall till he came runnin' out and away down the hall, the bloody sicko. You can be sure I locked the door after that when I'm getting changed if he's on duty."

"I see. Do you want to report him."

"No I'll leave it this time but if I catch him again I will."

"Right enough." I said, "I'll keep an eye on him when I can."

Time passed, he had now been with us a couple of months. As an officer, he was not so great, often going missing when needed and always making excuses to avoid any actual work.

This particular night was a very hot Summer night and unbeknown to us all he had found himself a quiet place to go for a snooze during the night: the storeroom where the spare beds and trolleys were kept, which was usually left undisturbed at night. As it was a very hot night he took a notion to strip off completely stark naked and covering himself with only a sheet, promptly lay down and went to sleep on one of the trolleys. As luck would have it, a couple of young nurses were dispatched urgently from casualty, to get a spare trolley. In they flustered into the semi-dark storeroom and immediately yanked the sheet off the nearest trolley. J.J. of course woke up with a screech and sat up. The young nurses also began screeching fit to lift the roof in fright. J.J. jumped off the trolley and ran towards them to try and calm them down, still naked. Of course all they saw in the dark room was a naked man running towards them and they ran screaming out of the room pursued by J.J. still trying to calm them down. As luck would have it, the no nonsense, burly matron was within ear shot of the doings, she seized a sweeping brush and arrived at a gallop to save her girls. Seeing what she immediately perceived to be a sex attacker she waded in, plying her brush with all the dexterity of a lethal stick fighting Ninja. She almost killed poor old J.J., who got hammered to the ground, begging for Mercy and help in alternate measure. The now prone J.J. was manhandled, or should I say woman handled, into the cleaning cupboard and locked therein until the Police arrived. They dragged him out none too gently. When it was finally established who he was it was all the guards could do to prevent the matron giving him another going over with the brush.

"Young man you are an obscene disgrace, get out of my hospital before I kill you, you sex fiend."

This last, she fairly spat at him. J.J. ran back into the storeroom, quickly put on his clothes and ran out of the hospital never to be seen again and thus ended his security career. First thing next morning she rang up the office and chewed one of our bosses for about twenty minutes before she went off duty. The other man on duty kept well out of her way that morning and slunk away home quietly when his shift ended.

Last time I heard of J.J. he was working in a porn shop in Dublin. He had found his vocation at last.

Chapter 9

A friend of mine got pole-axed guarding a building site. I asked him later what happened. He said. "I was walking around the site, it was getting dark and the last thing I remember was walking around the corner of a house. The next I remember I woke up on the ground with a very sore head. I was wobbling around a good while before I figured out what had happened and thought to call the supervisor and police."

There were some things stolen but nothing major. He was checked out in hospital and subsequently discharged after an x-ray. He made sure to have a torch, a baton, and a hard hat from then on while on duty on any other site. Of course by law we were not allowed to carry a baton or any means of defence or protection but the people who made such laws had not trudged around in darkness, in rough neighbourhoods, where poleaxing security guards was the best of fun, to some locals at least. So we carried batons. I knew of one fellow who was beaten to death years later after I had left that line of work. Ironically when I knew him he was not a security guard and I was. He was a nice enough fellow. But it was just a minor headline in a paper so I could get little more details on the matter than what the paper said, for I had lost touch with everyone by then.

On a lighter note again, a fellow was on duty on a hot day when one of the bosses arrived at the gate. In vain he blew his horn and banged on the gate. It was Sunday and nobody was expected. The portly director scaled the high gate and went to his offices, only to find the guard in the canteen, walking around in just his underpants, with music blasting from his stereo, stoned out of his head, singing at the top of his voice, jiggling around the kitchen trying to make himself a fry up of (bacon, eggs and sausages). The Director and he stared agape at each other for some minutes.

"I was a bit hot ya see....," he said at length.

The director grabbed his briefcase and bolted. The guard ran after him still in underwear, trying to explain. The director saw that he was being pursued and ran all the faster, and was over the gate much faster on the way out, into his shiny Mercedes and away like blazes on his road home. He did not come in on Sundays after that.

Another young fellow named Donal who was a bit of a head case was put on duty, in what was, then, a very tall office block. He went up on the roof to alleviate his boredom, where he came across an emergency fire hose. He turned on the tap, twisted the nozzle and, hey presto! It worked, a full jet of water. Looking out from atop the multi story office block, he started to pick targets, houses, other building and a load of people standing at a nearby bus stop, who didn't look up at all, they only started putting up umbrellas and hoods, huddling up as if in a bad shower. Garda cars were singled out, old ladies, mothers with prams, builders, anyone who came within range and nobody ever looked up. He had invented a new game. It did not occur to people to wonder why it was only raining on them. He said to me he had whiled away countless hours this way until he even got bored with this. Sometimes he just waited until the supervisor had gone and would lock the doors and head for the nearest pub. He did other bits of mischief, not documented here, before he finally left to return to college and finish whatever degree he was doing. I haven't seen him since and don't especially want to.

Chapter 10

At one stage on a particularly large site which was a quarry cum factory, the head officer on site did not have a car and spent a great deal of time pestering the office for a four wheel drive vehicle for use on site for driving around for himself. During an assessment from one of the office managers he got us all to say a four wheel drive was needed on site for our general use. On the face of it, this all seemed like a fairly good idea and it might even save us some shoe leather, as it was a very big site. At first the office was reluctant to trust us with a four wheel drive. Eventually however they did relent and gave us a Land Rover for the general disposal of the lads. We were all well pleased when our shiny green Land Rover arrived on site, things were looking up. Everybody had a go at driving it, trying to find out what was the roughest terrain they could drive it in and out of; up the side of hills, through fields, into boggy areas, through ditches, and so much more.

The weekend came and no one was around. Of course we were our usual well behaved selves. One of the directors had left his brand new black Mercedes parked outside his office for the weekend, to keep it safe.

"Yes indeed Mr Moylan you can count on us, we'll watch it like a hawk, don't worry at all." said a fawning Iggy to the director before he left.

"Good man it's a load off my mind, there have been a few cars vandalised around my area lately and I'm real proud of that car."

"So long now."

"Good luck now Mr Moylan don't worry about a thing. Enjoy your weekend."

The man drove away home in his less valuable car. Presently we all separated to do our various locking up and checking that all was in order. Dennis took the Land Rover to go and check the quarry, Iggy went to the factory and the yard, Roly headed for the warehouses and storage area, and myself and Dillon took the offices and the garage, locking doors, checking windows and setting alarms as we went. We all met two hours later to go and get a cup of tea. Me and Iggy were standing talking near the offices when we saw Dennis coming at us like a bat out of hell. We ran for our lives even though we knew he was only throwing a scare into us as a joke. We knew him too well to wait around. Of course he braked at the last minute, laughing madly, but the wheels were coated in muck from the fields, causing it to go into a wild skid. It shot across the car park and straight into the director's Mercedes, such a bang we heard. All five guards on duty stood and stared, our mouths open, nobody spoke, nobody could speak. At length Dennis, our formula one trainee, moaned, "Oh me fuckin' head! Holy Shit! Look at the feckin' Merc I'm a dead man."

He got out still rubbing his head. When we could talk we retrieved the Land Rover which was not too badly damaged. The Merc was a write-off, a meeting was called and ideas were sought.

"What'll we do lads? We'll all be sacked for this. Has anyone got any ideas?"

"Lets all fuckin' emigrate before we're arrested."

"Don't be stupid. Come on think will you."

And so we all thought...........and then we thought a bit more. Finally Roly who was always good at thinking outside the box came up with a plan. "Lets make it look like joy riders and do up a big report."

So we got one of our cars, drove it all over the lawns, outside the offices and left various ugly tyre tracks here and there. Then we got the Land Rover and did the same. Hey presto, a car chase, we scraped one of the doors of the offices to make it look like a break in, and I helped to draft one of the best bits of creative writing I had done in years. It began with us interrupting thieves who had driven in through the back fields while they were breaking into an office. We immediately gave chase, first they rammed the Land Rover, then as we pursued them they rammed the Merc as they were angry because we had interrupted them in the middle of their foul deed. One of us was injured in the process of course, to explain the lump on Dennis's forehead. It was a heroic battle of course, where they stopped to hurl missiles, abuse and made two fingered gestures at us, but we were not afraid and drove them back manfully. A copy of this was also put on the director's desk. We now placed all the ingredients in the oven and we waited... to be taken out and shot.

The first was a call from our boss in the security firm office confirming all details. Then more enquiries from the director. We all had our story straight and lied our asses off. After driving through the fields, we had driven along the road in a wide circle and back in the main gate leaving sets of tracks to the edge of the road way. Gardaí were called, we tracked the culprits with them to where the tracks ended at the edge of the road.

The cops offered us theories as to who it might be and where they went, we nodded sagely, obviously, they knew what they were about. Descriptions were proffered, vague descriptions: "Hoodies, baseball caps, it was dark, they were driving very fast. We were all a bit nervous."

Then as our shift had ended we all went home. The next time we came on duty the director came out to us and thanked us personally for saving the day and preventing a worse disaster, he gave us £20 each, said well done, and our boss even promoted our supervisor and gave us all a raise. There is probably a moral to this story, but I'm damned if I know what it is.

Eventually one weekend the Land Rover got bogged down in a field after some escapade or other, so when they failed to pull it out they got the bright idea of using one of the yard forklift trucks, not meant for soft ground, to try and lift it. They drove in forklift No. 1, which got to the spot but also got bogged down. They got forklift No.2 to try to pull out forklift No. 1 and even managed to get the forks under the Land Rover wrecking the under carriage in the process and then it got bogged down also. Forklifts 3, 4 & 5 also followed suit and of course come Monday morning there was one wrecked jeep and 5 forklift trucks stuck in the field. The whole delivery system turned to chaos in the yard with forty foot Lorries queuing out to the gate waiting to be loaded. The office was inundated with phone calls of irate customers screaming down the line looking for their deliveries. The drivers were going ballistic, the forklift drivers were going ballistic, the receptionists were threatening to quit if they got any more abuse over the phone, the bosses were getting chewed on from all sides.

They came out of their offices looking for blood and after finding out the cause and getting a large machine from the quarry to get out the forklifts, they proceeded to chew on the ears of our Boss, who promptly suspended two men, had the battered Land Rover removed from site never to be seen again or replaced and called us all into the office to shout and roar at us, even those of us who were not there like myself, for an hour before sending us on our way. The dust settled in a few weeks, things got back to normal and the episode was finally forgotten, thank heavens.

Chapter 11

I once worked on a building site which was a youth hostel being built not far from Dublin city. On the long trestle type benches someone had put polystyrene insulation sheets to sit on and I found it extremely comfortable to get my forty winks while on duty in the big site Porta-Cabin. The hours we did were so long we were always tired and the only way we could cope with them was to sleep while we could and when we could. Occasionally we were woken up by the noise of someone putting up posters outside on the timber hoarding around the site and excepting the supervisor we were usually left alone.

One night I was particularly tired, I put on the heater, took off my shoes, glasses and switched off the light. I left my baton, radio and torch on the trestle table, tied the guard dog to the leg of the big trestle table so that he guarded the open door. I then lay down and fell sound asleep. I was woken to a sound like thunder with the hut shaking, the guard dog growling and barking like a mad lion. All was noise and vibration in the pitch blackness. I sat up and actually screamed with fright. I could not find my glasses, my shoes, the radio, the torch or even get to the light switch. When I finally got my wits about me in the blackness, I found my glasses and finally the torch. I switched on the light and found my way out the door, blocked by the trestle table, the guard dog was still tied to the leg yowling and barking and lunging. I found my shoes, my radio, my baton and some of my wits. I managed to pull back the table to get out. I untied the dog and pushed back the table to where it had been, then, still shaking like a man having a fit, I did a full patrol of the site with the dog, baton, and torch. He growled and lunged into one of the doorways and out shot a cat with a mad screech, I almost died on the spot. Gradually I began to understand what had happened. I was asleep, the dog in the door way saw a cat walking by, he charged after it, being tied to the table he dragged it with him until it got caught in the doorway, knocking everything on the table and everything around the table all over the place and vibrating the hell out of the hut and scaring me so badly I nearly had a heart attack.

He wagged his big tail, "You stupid crazy bastard of a dickhead guard dog," I roared, "I almost bloody died of fright."

I was still shaking badly. I had babbled something incoherent into the radio to my supervisor who was on his way but I had to calm things down and say it was a false alarm without making myself look like too much of a fool. I'll tell you what I didn't say, I didn't say, "the guard dog saw a cat, I was sound asleep and when he woke me up trying to get at it, I nearly wet my pants with fright." No sir, I didn't say that. I was still shaking a bit when my shift ended and it was time to go home. From that night on, I never ever could fully relax, or sleep properly while on duty, even for a short nap. I would jump at the slightest noise, and sometimes I jumped at absolutely nothing. So much for my nerves of steel.

Chapter 12

I was on duty at the tennis club mentioned before and it was my wont, when I could, to use the gym at about 5 am to go for a swim in the pool and have a nice warm shower. I was just finished the shower, I was stark naked, towelling myself down, when I heard knocking. "Bloody hell," I thought, someone is early.

I looked up and to my horror there was a row of little heads of young school girls, all looking in at me from upper windows in the changing room, all looking delighted at seeing me. There was also one man looking none too happy.

"Shit, shit, shit," I muttered as I ran in the back to grab my uniform. They must have all been standing up on the bike rack outside the windows to see in. I grabbed my uniform and, dressing quickly, ran to the door still dripping wet, looking sheepish. A bunch of rich people's daughters were arriving for private tutoring from a professional tennis coach at 5 am. to finish and be ready in time for school the same morning.

Poor kids, as if school was not hard enough! They sure got some education that morning but I made sure I was not caught out again.

Sometime later that month, I was back on duty at the quarry and I found a car that had recently been stolen by local joy riders. It had been rallied around the fields and upended upside down in a ditch at the back of the quarry. Usually, they set the cars alight. Maybe I had interrupted them. Anyhow, rooting around in the debris I found some details of the owner strewn around the field. I rambled up to the main gate to use the phone. I rang a number I had found. It went like this: "Hello, is your name Mr. John Black?"

"Yes."

"Do you own a car, a blue Ford SI 4386?"

"Yes."

"Well, I'm a security guard with Rondale Quarries in Foxton. Has your car been stolen?"

"No, I don't think so." Then, "Hold on, I'll see."

Pause. Footsteps.

In the distance, "Holy Fuck!"

Footsteps back to phone. Sounding depressed, "I think it might be mine."

He arrived some time later with a friend. I brought them to the scene of devastation. There was no doubting who the owner was; he looked as if he were going into shock. He spoke to me with a vague far away voice, his eyes never leaving his poor savaged car and his bits and pieces around the field. He looked so lost you just felt like giving him a hug and saying "there, there, it'll be alright son, you'll get over this," but I just said I was sorry about his car and left him to grieve in peace. Poor chap. I haven't much sympathy for criminals because I have seen too much of their handiwork up close. I suppose that was a minor thing compared to some of the things I had seen and heard. But it was nevertheless a heart breaking event for that young man.

Now and again we got a new recruit who was, if it was possible, an even bigger headcase than we were. Enter Fearless Freddy as we called him, with whom I only had the briefest of conversations. I don't know who interviewed him but they must have been taking some special drugs that morning when they gave him the job. During our very brief conversation he kept saying things to me about "going to the frontline" and "stepping into the combat zone."

I think he mistakenly thought that he had joined some army platoon heading for a new war in Vietnam or something similar. I mean being a bit out there sometimes had its advantages, when you were bored mindless, wandering around like a dickhead in your ratty uniform, trying to look important. But when they gave him the job as a plain clothes store detective in a major supermarket complex, without proper training or instruction. Now that took a special talent where judgement was concerned, on our employer's part. Perhaps he mistook the mad gleam in his eye for enthusiasm for the job. In a way, he might have been right, as there was definitely enthusiasm of a sort.

He showed up on time alright, in full combat gear, presumably acquired in some army surplus store. I don't know if Khaki is the proper name for the green and black variety, topped by a black beret worn at a rakish tilt. The first time the staff became aware of him was when they spotted this guy ducking in and out from behind pillars in the shop and sneaking in and out from behind shelves, now and again flattening himself against a wall, presumably to avoid bullets; stalking around after various customers. Every now and again muttering something in his radio, stuff like: "I'm watching this old woman here, she might be going to steal something."

"This couple looks suspicious, I'm moving to a new location to reconnoitre the situation."

"I might have to apprehend this young girl if she doesn't pay for that bar of chocolate...not to worry I have my own handcuffs..."

The girl in our radio control room thought it was one of us acting the fool, as we sometimes did and would not answer, but this guy was not acting. The staff and the customers were getting a bit scared and contacted our uniformed people who were also working in the centre.

"There's some lunatic in a soldier's uniform runnin' around in here, frightenin' the life out of everyone, can yez come down and get him out."

When they came to collect him and realized who he was and what he was supposed to be doing, it was very hard to keep a straight face.The staff of the store were not amused and the irate manageress rang our boss to chew his head off.

"May I ask are you now selecting your officers from the local mental home?"

"What's the idea of sendin' in 'Rambo' to frighten the life out of my customers and staff? Do you think that's funny? Because we don't, we thought he had a gun and was goin' ta' kill us all. I don't know why you're bloody laughin', I can have you removed and replaced very quickly indeed... Saying sorry is fine but if it happens again you're out of here, good day to you."

The poor fellow was moved around a bit from one location to another and eventually had to be let go as he was a bit too far gone, even for our screwy outfit

Chapter 13

A friend of mine was on duty in the coal yard. He liked to dabble in anything that would either get him drunk or stoned, particularly when on duty. He said it made the night go quicker, as you could well see how it would. I remember once being relieved of duty by him in said coal yard and watched in amazement as he took out his "lunch." It consisted of a large bottle of vodka, topped up with orange juice, two six packs of beer and two ounces of hash.

"D'ya think that'll last me for the night Jimmy?" he said, proud of his little stash.

I said I imagined it might keep him on a different planet for a few days at least.

He laughed, delighted with himself. "Ring me later for a chat," he said.

I said I would. When I did ring later he was well advanced into inebriation, or some form of 'out there' experience. He said "I'm sorry Jimmy, I can't talk now, there's something really crazy happening, Man its great...you wouldn't believe it." So saying, he hung up. He had sounded like a man hanging on to a lovely dream.

Anyhow, back to the original story. He was on duty on this occasion. Someone of his friends had supplied him with a hundred "magic mushrooms," that is mushrooms that have a hallucinogenic effect, nature's drugs. He chopped them up small, mixed them up with some lemonade and downed the lot.

He told me later "I just remember sitting there thinking these mushrooms aren't much use. Next I remember there were seagulls screeching over me head and waves near me. I couldn't figure out where I was until I recognised the lighthouse and then I had to walk all the way back and it was feckin' freezing." It transpired that he had somehow managed to walk three miles to a remote lighthouse out along a causeway in a sort of trance and when he did come around he had a long walk back. Oh the incredible power of a little mushroom. I think he stuck to the hash and booze after that.

I came on duty one Saturday afternoon, only to find my fellow officer with a guard dog tied to a lamp post while he belted him with the sweeping brush. The dog was going berserk.

"What are you doing Eddie?" I exclaimed.

"The fucker ate all me sandwiches I had for the night, I'll kill 'um" he replied.

"For God's sake stop hitting him, I'll share my sandwiches with you."

"Yeah?" he said, now petulant. "But they were me favourite fresh chicken and this shithead dog ate them all."

So saying, he hit him again.

"Eddie, stop, ya' silly bastard, that's a guard dog, not a poodle. We have to work with him after this. He'll kill you for that if he gets the chance and you won't be worried about your fucking sandwiches then. Go on try and untie him now if you're able."

He paused, thoughtful then, eyeing the dog as he continued to lunge at him.

I continued, "What'll you do if we have a break-in and you have to go after these guys without a dog?"

"Oh..." he said.

But it was too late, the dog hated him forever more and never forgot. It almost got him once, but that's another story.

In truth the poor dogs were often half starved and beaten and abused, small wonder they were all a bit mental, a bit like us. It was common enough for guard dogs to pinch your sandwiches from your work bag, if they got the chance or you left it near them. But it was a long night for us too, if we had no food to eat for sixteen hours, so I understood where Eddie was coming from too. It's hard to be right sometimes.

Chapter 14

Still on doggies, I remember a guy who was forever being caught asleep. The supervisor had said if he caught him again he'd be sacked. So while he was on the phone to me he told me of his great plan. He said "There's no way I can stay awake all night. What I'll do is bring the guard dog into the hut and tie the lead onto my leg and when the supervisor arrives the dog will wake me up."

Well, he wasn't wrong. The supervisor arrived at 4 am. Jason was sound asleep, but the dog was wide awake in a jiffy. He thought it was the dog van to collect him and he shot out the door of the guard hut to greet the driver. Jason was yanked off the chair by the leg and walloped his head so hard off the floor he was almost knocked out. He was summarily dragged across the floor and only his big frame got caught in the doorway he would have been dragged down a flight of stone steps outside the hut, being walloped all the way down. He writhed around on the floor trying to get the lead off his leg with the dog pulling like mad. Eventually after a desperate struggle he managed to undo the lead and release the animal that ran to the gate. The supervisor noticed nothing except to ask why the dog was loose.

"Oh he must have pulled free of that thing I tied him to."

"I see," he replied. As he was leaving, he caught a glimpse of the back of Jason's uniform. "Good grief Jason, look at the back of your uniform, what were 'ya doin' rollin' around the floor or somethin'?"

"Yeah, ha, ha, rollin' around the floor"....

I can still recall vividly, when, either on festive occasions like Christmas or Easter or at weekends, especially long weekends when there would be a bank holiday on Monday, going into work for the night; envying all the young people dressed in their finery heading out to socialize and enjoy themselves. I felt like a condemned man going off to jail. Sometimes the nightshifts were sixteen hours long and I would become morose and depressed hating my lot, thinking to myself how shit life was; unfair and sickening. I had to work these long unsociable hours and I, a single man in my prime, or so I thought, to keep my mortgage paid, while the rest of the world was out 'on the tear'.

I myself, at that time was not adverse to an occasional drinking session and even perhaps, not to put too fine a point on it, 'chasing an odd bit of skirt'. Nights like this, going into work, started off badly and only seemed to get worse, as the long night shift wore on and on and on... When I arrived on site the man on duty, not believing his luck to be off on such a night, would only deliver to me the most perfunctory of conversation and would be out the gate and gone, in a manner reminiscent of that old cartoon character 'the Roadrunner' minus the 'Beep! Beep!' I would stare forlornly after his departing figure with a woe begotten look in my eyes wishing it was me instead of him. The location I was on would usually be some dirty and depressing shithole in some dangerous part of Dublin, where, if you did fall asleep, it was best to sleep very lightly indeed, lest one be pole-axed with a blunt instrument while asleep. Often I was in the middle of some vast, mucky building site, in the middle of nowhere, the environs of which was populated by individuals who on occasion could indeed be detrimental to a security guard's health, as getting the living shit kicked out of oneself can indeed be a harrowing business. Their favourite hobbies included stealing, taking drugs and of course driving stolen cars at high speed, sometimes at us. So it was best to remain alert at all times.

And, I hear you say, "what did this intrepid, brave security guard do when a car laden with drug crazed or drunken teenagers, coming out of nowhere, a stolen car, bore down on him at high speed, while he was doing his rounds?" Well that's a no brainer really. I, of course, ran like the proverbial rabbit, clearing fences and walls in the process, in a manner worthy of a champion racehorse in the Grand National, in a most sincere effort to stay alive and get to a phone or a chance to use my radio, if I had one, to call someone, preferably the police, to come and save my sorry ass, while same was still in my possession.

The worst times were often these self same weekends or festive occasions when these people were high on drugs, drunk or simply bored and angry with the world in general.

One such location had me so frightened that I borrowed a small crossbow from a friend and took to bringing it to work with me for a while and I carried it around with me loaded and with the safety off while doing my rounds.

I almost shot the supervisor on one occasion, who foolishly, was trying to sneak up on me in the dark or catch me asleep. Fortunately he was unaware as to how close he had come to getting a little surprise himself, as I had stashed the implement before approaching him. I greeted him out of the darkness shining my torch in his face. I was now unarmed and smiling. Still, I was somewhat gratified that I scared the daylights out of him. He looked like he had just wet his trousers, though of course, still oblivious as to how close he had actually come to a warrior's grave himself.

Here I must stress some supervisors were the best and decent guys to boot. Here, however, stood a Bona fide, card carrying prick. He was one of those annoying little dickheads who, with very limited experience in security work, presumed he could outflank lads like myself, who had endured all manner of crap to last this long. We had seen his ilk come and go while we had worked all kinds of hours, in all kinds of weather, in all kinds of situations: some pretty hairy, twenty four hours a day, every day, year in year out. He had no particular intelligence to speak of. He was a sneak and a telltale. I felt sure he would go far in the Irish security industry, providing of course, that I did not shoot the little bastard first.

Chapter 15

I remember one Christmas, I and an ex-army chap were on duty in a hotel on the north side of the city. He was working in another section, but we both got together in the hotel. We sat depressed, lamenting that everyone was out celebrating except us: poor fools working nights. We looked at the bar all shuttered up.

"I wouldn't mind a pint, would you?" said he.

"I sure wouldn't" said I.

Lenny started to examine the shutters closely and somehow figured how to unbolt one of them from the outside. Up went the shutters and it was drinks all round. The supervisor arrived. It was Benny. Benny was alright, but supervisor is supervisor. Down went the shutters, glasses hidden.

"Well Benny," we said.

"How are yez lads?"

He produced two bottles of beer, one each, to cheer us up. Myself and Lenny exchanged a glance and nodded.We let him in on the secret. Drinks all round again. We even sang a few songs as the night wore on. When Benny eventually did go, it was a very wobbly Benny indeed. He missed half his calls that night, but, what the hell, it was Christmas anyway, wasn't it?

Lenny and I kept quiet about it to our respective relief officers, who must have wondered how we could be so jolly after a long night shift. We made it home somehow. Both had fairly good hangovers when we did manage to wake up to go out for our next shift. Lenny was married. I was single and living alone. So it didn't really matter how drunk I got, or how often but while I did enjoy an occasional splurge I was not a very big drinker by comparison with many of my friends. But then I suppose that would not be saying much, considering half of them were alcoholics or training hard to qualify as one. But life was a dull business if it was just work alone. So we made the best of every opportunity for a bit of relief from constant monotony. After all you only live once.

On duty in the tennis club again, I was starting another long night shift. The last of the V.I.P. members had wobbled out the door at 1 a.m., into their posh cars and away home as drunk as monkeys. The bar staff were cleaning up behind the bar. I was doing a ramble around the building doing my security bit: checking emergency exits were locked, that all inebriated souls had left the building i.e. no prone bodies lying in corners under tables or in toilets; no smouldering cigarettes or cigars on the carpet or on the seats; no windows left open lest an opportunistic intruder gain access to the premises. Open windows would also trip the alarm when it was set and other riveting stuff like that I could mention but I won't; spare you all I shall.

I was feeling mighty sorry for myself as usual, lost in deep thought and down in the dumps.

"Jim," said a familiar voice.

"Yes," said I looking all around.

It was the pretty little barmaid Molly talking to me through the hatch at the end of the counter.

"How are you Molly?"

"Grand Jim, do you fancy a pint?"

"Does a cat drink milk?" I thought to myself.

Aloud I said, "A pint of ale would be lovely Molly thanks."

Although I really thought that she was messing until the pint actually appeared in the hatch.

"There you go Jim."

"Fair play to you Molly thanks a million."

I sat down at a table in the lounge to enjoy my pint not believing my luck. Presently all four bar staff came out to join me, all with drinks in hand. There were two barmen and two barmaids, a likeable enough bunch. I looked at my watch it was about 1.15 a.m., my supervisor would not be around until after 7 a.m. I was then a single man, I did not live far away, I was travelling by bicycle so I was safe enough and boy did I love a good piss-up. So lucky them they had picked the right man for the occasion.

The bit of chat began, as chats often do. More drinks, a few jokes, a few laughs, more drinks, the night progressed, songs were sung, more drinks. I stood up and bawled out some song I knew. I got a big clap. The two lads sang a duet, another clap, the girls did the same, big clap, we all sang one together, more drinks. I did a radio check while I could still speak normally, more drinks. We turned on some loud music and Stella the other girl did a sexy dance for us all on a table and fell off half way through. We all laughed fit to bust including the girl on the floor. This was promising to be no ordinary night; more drinks. Next I knew Molly was sitting on my lap, bouncing up and down, giggling her head off, well and truly sloshed, as was I. The two lads had procured a football from somewhere, using two barstools for goalposts and with Stella in goal they were trying to score goals against the back wall of the lounge. I liked a good kickabout as good as anybody, but drunk as I was there was no way I was missing my chance with Molly, if this was a chance. Sure enough, next I knew I was snogging her in a corner with my hand inside her blouse (could I be dreaming? Who cares? Dream on.)

But my adventures with Molly got no further, worse luck 5 a.m. came, everyone was tired and drunk, including me. They pulled me another pint and said.

"Jimmy you're the best crack on a piss-up we ever had. You're a complete mental case and no mistake. We love ya Jimmy goodnight ya headcase."

"I love yez all as well, fair play to yez it was a grand little session we had, safe home now."

"We'll see you when you're on duty again."

I never did get any further with Molly. Oh the fickleness of women. Still we all remained friendly just the same. Occasionally they would drop me a pint before they went home, but we never had a session like that again. Understandably, they did not want to risk losing their jobs if we were caught. Still it lifted my spirits that night and cheered me up no end: a timely and unexpected piss-up is a treat indeed. Locking the front door I went back to the lounge and collapsed onto one of the seats into a sound sleep. I was awoken by my supervisor hammering on the door who berated me for taking so long to answer the door.

"Were ya in a coma or somethin?" (Close enough.)

But it was Benny my old friend, so things were cool. I imagine the smell of alcohol on my breath would have curled his hair if he actually had any, but he didn't, so lucky him. I'm sure he must have noticed my dishevelled state, but he said nothing and neither did I. We chatted a while and he left, my head was thumping and I set about sobering up: drinking tea, washing face, combing hair, rinsing mouth out, straightening up my crumpled uniform and generally making myself presentable. None of the clubhouse staff or members were early that morning as if they had, they might have been less charitable than Benny, but I guess I was on a bit of a roll on that particular shift and so I say also, lucky me.

I went home that morning, collapsed into bed, had a sound sleep and was back on duty that night, in a horrible, mucky building site on the opposite side of town, surrounded by a great many antisocial types. Such types being, as I said before, not overly enamoured of security guards and they were all dead shots with stones. I was paying for my sins of the night before and doubtless keeping my head very low indeed, ya can't win 'em all.

James Linnane

Chapter 16

Gerry was the opposite of Barney, a decent and honest fellow, always on time, always sober and in good humour. Like Stevie, I liked him a lot. He was one of the old crew, and like us he was a long time with the firm. But if ever a man was bedevilled by disaster, it was surely Gerry. He weighed about twenty stone; he was a big, overweight harmless poor old devil.

A couple of episodes involving him and the dogs:

Guard dogs are big dogs and when you walk them, some of them really pull on the leash; like holding onto a small team of huskies after shouting "Mush" they nearly pull your arms off.

One morning Gerry was coming back off a patrol with a dog called "Dax" on the lead. The dog van arrived at the main gate of the site. This meant back to the kennel and above all, food. He pulled wildly, speeding Gerry up to a trot, then a fast trot, then an uncontrollable run. He stumbled and fell face down in the deep muck. The lead was wrapped around his wrist and he was unceremoniously dragged for the last twenty yards face down, losing his glasses in the process, before he could free himself, letting the dear doggie gallop the last few yards alone. The dogman saw Gerry rise up like 'the beast from the black lagoon', covered from head to toe in muck, and did not trust himself to speak, shaking with mirth, with poor Gerry gazing at him coldly, daring him to laugh.

He told me he drove down the road, pulled in and laughed for twenty minutes solid. "Even though I did feel sorry for Gerry but Jimmy, ya' just had to be there. It was the funniest thing I ever seen."

On another occasion on the site, the builders had dug huge holes on the site about eight feet deep, which immediately filled up with rainwater. Gerry was out patrolling with another lively guard dog called 'Dancer'. When they got to one of the holes full of water, Dancer thought "Goody, play time" and jumped in. Unfortunately, Gerry, still wrapping the lead around his wrist, could not let go quickly enough and he followed the dog into the water. I arrived to relieve him later that day. He had bits of muck on him, still dripping and sodden, his teeth chattering.

"How did you manage to get out?"

"I nearly didn't."

His last misfortune was a classic; you really just couldn't invent this stuff. He was on duty in a yard for industrial gas cylinders, you know, acetylene, oxygen, propane and such. The thing was, every evening we would arrive on duty, the staff would lock the gate as they left with us inside the yard. Later on, our supervisor would drop us his key, which he would collect in the morning before he went home. At eight o'clock the staff would arrive, unlock the gate and we were free to go home. However, it had no toilet, so if you wanted to have a crap before you got the key, you had to climb the eight foot high fence topped with spikes and barbed wire to go to the workman's club next door; no mean feat when you were built like Gerry. He got out alright, had his poo, and was climbing back in when he slipped. The leg of his uniform trousers snagged on the top of the fence and he was left dangling and squawking. The uniforms we had at that time were old Garda uniforms, you almost couldn't rip them. So, dangling and squawking was poor old Gerry. Meanwhile in the workman's club the booze was flowing and everyone was in great form. Someone looked out a window and spotted poor old Gerry.

"Help....help..." said Gerry.

One called another to the window and they all lined up at the window jeering, laughing and pointing.

"Help me!" said Gerry.

The people in the worker's club, men and women, couldn't believe their luck. This was the best laugh they'd had in years.

"Help."

The more he shouted the more they howled with laughter. Eventually, a little fellow came staggering out of the clubhouse towards Gerry. As the little drunk came near, Gerry felt relieved,

"Oh thank God! I thought nobody was going to help me."

But the little fellow just ran up, gave Gerry a good kick in the arse and ran back into the clubhouse cackling. The audience howled with laughter.

Finally, the trousers did rip and Gerry managed to get down without breaking his neck, somehow. Poor old Gerry.

Chapter 17

Then there were the litany of tragedies which befell my fellow officers: One fellow in his late twenties got a phone call at work telling him his wife had dropped dead from a brain haemorrhage, leaving him with five children to raise on his own. Another man a bit older, his wife died of a heart attack, leaving him with four children one of them handicapped. One young chap, engaged to be married, was diagnosed with cancer, had his testicles removed and months of chemotherapy, losing all of his hair for a time. When he had come through all of this he did get married. Most of his family later got cancer of some sort and his younger brother, who also worked for us for a time, shot himself with a shotgun. A young fellow I worked with briefly, a nice enough chap, got sacked for something minor and drove in front of a double decker bus the following week. Whether deliberate or accidental – no one knows. Either way he died.

Another fellow's wife went off her head and wound up in a mental home, apparently she was quite a brilliant poet. Again he was left coping with a handicapped son. Though he and I did not like each other, I would never have wished him that kind of misfortune.

A friend of mine, a bit too fond of fights and brawling in pubs and such, got knocked out in a row in a late night take away, when someone procured a metal mop handle from the floor mop in the corner and bent it over his head. A lump developed as a result and turned out to be cancer over time and in spite of treatment it almost took his life.

My own 17 year old nephew shot himself and as I had been quite close to him it left me reeling for some time to come, years perhaps. Even now it still seems fresh in my mind, after all this time. A young fellow whose girlfriend left him, and whose best friend working in England dropped dead at twenty four from a heart attack, had a nervous breakdown and wound up in a mental institution. Tragedies and misfortunes seemed to come from nowhere when they were least expected. A seasoned veteran in his fifties was enjoying his Christmas dinner with his family when he had a heart attack and died.

A friend of mine had lost his job and was about to hang himself. He rang me to say goodbye, "You were the only friend I had whenever I was in trouble, I just wanted to say goodbye and thanks Jim..... for everything. Its time for me to go, bye bye!!."

Sleepy as I was I woke up fast. I kept him talking,

"Nothing is worth that, you're still young and your whole life is before you. Don't give up so soon. There's plenty more good days ahead."

"But Jimmy I can't take anymore, I'm just fucked..." So saying he started to cry.

"Luke will you hang on till I get there and we'll have a chat about this. Sure we can work this out between us. Will ya' wait for me Luke, will ya now?"

"I will Jim"

"Now ya' wont let me down, ya' will hang on won't you?"

"I will"

"Swear ya' will"

"I will"

"Good man"

I had no car at that time, so as I lived some miles away I had to phone a taxi. I got there told the taxi to wait, he let me in. I put my arm around him and he cried on my shoulder for about twenty minutes."You'll be alright now, Lukey boy, you'll be alright now..." I murmured.

He had wet his trousers with fear of what he was about to do. The noose was made from a flex at the back of the t.v., hanging from the steel bar off his weights which he put across the open attic trap door. Undoubtedly it would have worked. I dismantled it, put his coat on him and brought him home with me in the taxi. I settled him with a can of beer and a chat, gave him a change of clothes for the morning and sent him to bed. I got a few hours myself before I had to go to work. A house I was trying to rent needed redecorating so I set him to work and paid him any way I could and I worked with him when I could. It took a couple of weeks during which he stayed with me. He was still a bit unsteady emotionally, but he had turned a corner. He'd be alright now. Presently he moved out and four years later when I had lost touch with him, his brother told me Luke was now general manager of a large hotel in Dublin city, and I was the one now struggling to find a job. But I didn't bother him; I was glad for him and glad to have done something good for once. But for now I was still beavering away doing security work. I was on a large building site on a hill with my friend Eddie, it was about 4am and so very dark and cold. We decided to go out on patrol through the large building under construction. We were expecting our relatively new supervisor to call any hour now. He was a sneaky little rat who tried hard to catch us asleep so that he could report us to our boss, so he was not well liked. We rambled along chatting with "Roy" the guard dog trotting ahead of us in the dark. Suddenly the dog launched into the darkness and disappeared. Next thing there was fierce growling and barking and someone screaming, "Get off me ya' bastard, Help! help! I'll be killed.....save me."

We ran to see, shining the torch, only to see it was the supervisor pinned to the ground. Roy had his teeth sunk in his arm. He had been so intent on catching us asleep, he forgot about the dog and sneaked over the fence and in through the building like a thief. We hauled the dog off him and brought him into the hut to disinfect and bandage his arm with the first aid kit. He whinged and gave out to us all the while and said we deliberately set the dog on him, which we didn't, though we might have liked to. He eventually went on his way and me and Eddie laughed our heads off.

"What a dumb asshole," said Eddie.

"You took the words right out of my mouth Edward. Fancy a cup of tea."

"Don't mind if I do James old boy."

The supervisor stopped climbing fences for a while after that but he was still a moron. I suppose if we liked him we might have been more sympathetic to his plight, but we didn't and he didn't like us either, so there you have it. Never the twain shall meet.

Chapter 18

I was on duty with Buster on a big site, it was a well known company which had gone wallop, shafting many of its loyal employees who had served them for years. It was a very big site and its offices were huge. The river nearby had recently burst its banks and flooded all houses and businesses in the area, including the ground floor of the main offices of the building we were guarding, covering all in river sludge, which was foul indeed. It dried to a very fine powdery dust to a depth of a few inches and when we walked through it we sent up little clouds of dust around our feet as we walked. Buster loved his nice new car, some kind of hatchback. He cleaned it inside and out, and minded it as if it were a baby. Buster was from Kimmage, not the worst I suppose, likeable enough, but shifty at best and at worst downright untrustworthy. But we got along. I suppose Buster's philosophy was that if it wasn't nailed down..... Buster was interested especially if it could fit in the boot of his car. From the early days working with Buster, I noticed he could settle himself anywhere in all weathers and be asleep in five minutes, sound asleep in a cardboard box, on a chair, on the floor in the car, I mean anywhere.

One day we came back from patrol and decided to have a cup of tea. Buster said "I left me bag in the car I'll get it."

The guard dog was loose and trotting beside us as I went with him. He got to the car and remembered Prince who loved riding in cars any chance he got: open the door and he was in. Buster eyed him and his mucky paws and said "if you think you're getting in my car you have another thing comin' ya' hoor' ya'."

So saying he opened the door at lightning speed grabbed his bag and closed it again.

"Ha, ha," said Buster "you're not quick enough for me."

He turned to look at the guard dog who was not there, "Where'd he go?"

I was just able to point holding back the laughter. He turned to see Prince sitting in the back seat of his locked car looking out waging his tail. Buster went mental but he knew better than to hit a guard dog trained to attack."Ya' mangy fleabittin' mutt, if I had a gun I'd shoot ya', ya rotten little hoor, look at me bleedin' car, will ya'."

Sure enough it was a mess but the dog didn't mind, he just wagged his tail. As quick as Buster had been, the dog had moved like greased lightning, he moved like a blur so quick was he. Buster cleaned the mess as best he could giving out all the way.

So after a cup of tea and a sandwich we went for another patrol around the front, which had a big field fronted by railings. The grass in the field had been neglected and had grown long. It was a favourite area for local cats to gather. Prince shot into the grass at lightning speed grabbed a cat killed it and turned managing to get a second one before he could get away. Then he picked them up one by one and dropped them at our feet. Buster thought it was hilarious but I wasn't laughing, they were someone's pet. Sure enough a few nights in succession an old lady next door was to be heard, "Here kitty, kitty, kitty," rattling his / her food bowl.

She lived alone, he was probably her only friend in the world. Night after night she would call till she must have realised he was not coming home. My conscience gave a twang but what could I do? We let the guard dog run loose because he needed the exercise. If you held him on the leash he wore you out pulling against you; if you tied him to a pole he bit through the lead. If you locked him in a room he would crap and stink the place up. Sometimes we were given dog boxes, usually not.

One Summer evening as we came around the front, there was an American tourist with a big behind, sitting at the railings, his posterior against the railing waiting for a bus. I didn't notice him but Prince did. He shot over and nipped him hard. The poor American shrieked jumped up and ran to the sanctuary of his friends. I leashed the dog as quick as I could and retreated, seeing the fellow rubbing his ample behind telling his friends, "Man that goddamn dog just bit me on the ass."

"So much for diplomatic relations with you around Prince; killing cats, biting tourists. What's next?" He wagged his big tail.

In those days I was a bit of a workaholic. I would work six and seven days a week. Sometimes I would leave one job and go to another. If I wasn't in security work I was doing bar work, I was a shop assistant or working in construction. By chance there was a well known politician, a nice enough fellow, whose wife was a well known T.V. personality, both of whom I knew well from my bar work days. Well it transpired that he would keep running into me: behind the counter in various places, his local shop getting his newspaper, his local pub buying his pint, the car park where he parked his car. I would say "Hello Michael."

He would say in his aristocratic accent, "By jove you work here too do you?" We'd chat for a little while and he would go.

A fellow officer was ill one day and I had to fill in for him, and wouldn't you know it, the shift was monitoring the front desk where Michael worked. He subsequently came in to the foyer where I was on duty, I said "Hello again Michael."

He looked visibly shocked exclaiming loudly, "Good lawd surely not you again, you're bloody everywhere."

And so I was. At that time I certainly did get around. I hadn't much of a social life at that time. I lived alone and at work getting paid, was as good as any place for me to be, back then.

Chapter 19

At one stage, particularly in Dublin, the airwaves were full of pirate radio stations and it wasn't to say that some of them were not fairly crap and unprofessional, but it was the selection and the lack of blandness, which is in all the media today that set them apart. You knew that local radio meant local radio. You never knew what might happen or be said on air: some of it brilliant, some of it awful and some hilarious. Sometimes, people showing up drunk and swearing on the airwaves. Playing incredible music telling the wives to have the dinner ready they'd be home in an hour, on air, or saying things like, "Tracey did you rob me bleedin' sandwich ya' wagon, I'm bleedin starvin'," or, "You're some slapper showin' me your knockers and me on air."

Rows, insults, madness and more. For people like us, who were working nights, it was a godsend as it kept us from going mad with boredom. But our government saw a chance to make money, licensing these radio stations and so they passed laws to close all the pirate stations down and that is what happened on the 30th December 1988 at midnight: they had to all go off air. I remember how utterly miserable I felt as they all shut down one by one. I even wrote a miserable poem to say how miserable I was. It's ok, I'll spare you all having to read it. All that remained on air was R.T.E's Radio 2 and it wasn't a patch on the pirate radio stations and it never would be. Perhaps it was their complete lack of discipline and inhibitions that made the pirates better. Even though many of their D.J's transferred to R.T.E and other licensed channels later on, somehow they left their fire and frivolity behind when they transferred.

I was in a dark dreary coal yard that night along the docks, with the sea wind howling in to further compound my miseries. It was dreary, isolated and dark, and patrolling it in the dark was just no fun at all. It could make the bravest man nervous. So it was, I rambled down the yard past the sheds, down towards the back end of the yard. As I rounded the corner I heard voices. It was pitch black and although some dock workers worked late, none were expected at 3am.

Over by the quay wall I could see a couple of silhouettes. They were loading bags of coal into a row boat. The water was rough, it looked dangerous. What should I do? Should I run and phone the police or should I just confront them? "What are you doing there?," I shouted shining my lamp on them.

One fellow, a big portly fellow, was standing up in the boat holding a bag of coal. I had a baton but no guard dog. His partner in crime had just gotten into the boat. The craft was a bit over laden. The waves were rough. The sudden light in his eyes unmanned the big fellow and he staggered with his load and falling into the water he managed to overturn the boat in the process. Both men went into the water screaming with fright. The big fellow broke the surface and was thrashing about like a maniac, "Help, help! I can't fuckin' swim, gurgle!, gurgle!... I can't... hep... Gurgle! gurgle!"

I made a decision and took a chance. There was a life ring on a rope on the wall. I grabbed it and threw it to him, he grabbed it and I hauled him in. He got onto the quay and lay there retching and panting. His comrade was clinging to the upturned boat which was starting to sink. "Grab hold young fella'!" I roared over the wind.

I threw the ring again. He grabbed as the boat sank. I dragged him up the steps. He was lighter than the other fellow.

When big boy got his breath back he said, "What did ya' hafta' shine that light in my eyes for?"

"Because I'm a feckin' security guard, that's what I'm paid for, or do you think I wear this uniform for fancy dress?"

"Are you okay young lad?" I asked the other fellow who was

coming around a bit.

"Yeah, thanks," he said wiping his runny nose on his wet sleeve.

"Well what'll you do now, call the police?" said the big one.

"No, I don't think so, I'll put in my report that ya got away, you've had enough torture for one night. I'll radio this in, in a few hours."

"Fair play to ya and thanks for savin' us. I thought robbin' coal by boat was clever, now I know."

"Will ya be able to make it home alright the two of ya."

"Yeah, we'll be alright, it's not too far, pity bout the 'oul boat.....come on Joey, your Ma will bleedin' skin me for this."

The sodden pair trudged off down the road in the freezing wind. I called it in later on, much later on, details were changed and the boat did not sink in my report. I said I was too late and they got clean away. Everyone needs a break now and again.

At around that time, though in truth, I can't be sure of the dates, there was a rapist who was active in Dublin and all women understandably were frightened to go out alone. He would jump on them in alleyways, attack them in their cars. Day or night, you never knew when or where he would strike next.

Well it happened that a couple of our boys were on duty in a car park in the south city area when one of them spotted a man jump into a car beside a woman going out in a queue of cars. He was holding something to her throat which transpired to be a piece of broken glass. The guard radioed his comrade and they both ran to the car, yanked open the door and dragged him out by the hair. "Let me go yez bastards or I'll kill yez."

But a good kick in the balls knocked some of the fight out of him. He was unceremoniously thrown to the ground and sat on while the police were called. They presently arrived and arrested him. Later at the station he was admitted to a number of other attacks on women and he was nicked.

It was mostly by a lucky co-incidence that our officers happened to spot him and take in the significance of the man's actions. Of course, if they had not reacted so promptly, things could have been much different for that woman and other subsequent victims of this man.

The man was given a long jail sentence and there were no further assaults at that time. It is to the credit of the officers in question who were gutsy enough to have a go. Sometimes that's all it takes, a little luck and a bit of courage.

Chapter 20

Denny was a likable fellow of small stature, who joined us as a supervisor. A nice guy and no mistake! He never cursed, didn't drink much, devoted himself to Jesus and generally worked very hard. It transpired he was a real Mormon minister. Well now, there was a surprise. He even performed marriage ceremonies. He was starting to get our attention. He was an entirely new species to us. All us good, mostly catholic boys whose favourite hobbies were drinking, fighting, shagging (when we got the chance) any woman we could, swearing constantly and many were worse thieves than some in jail. Yes, good old Denny had come to the right place. He had truly found a bunch of sinners in need of saving. This was a great fascination to us.

Of course, the first chance we got the interrogation began, "Tell us Denny what's the story with ye lads havin' a load a wives? Fond of the 'oul fanny are yez?"

Poor Denny would patiently explain the conditions which allowed a Mormon to "care for" another man's wife when or if he died and how it dated back to the early settlers and pioneers in America where a woman alone would have difficulty surviving "unprotected." It didn't wash with our listeners. "Go way outta that, you're not in the Wild West now, yez are just mad for fanny like the rest of us. How d'yez do any work when yez have to go home and shag two or three women? D'yez not be too tired? Come to think of it, why d'yez bother coming to work at all?"

We were all quite disappointed when we found out he had only one wife. This was getting interesting. "Would ya never think of getting' another one, ya know a nice fit young wan about sixteen or seventeen, nice an' fresh. Ya could send us a few nude pictures ta' show us what we're missin' not bein' Mormons like." Denny's face was getting red, the poor fellow was out of his depth. I think he thought he had come face to face with Lucifer himself.

My friend continued, "Us Catholics can only have one bleedin' wife. Mind you Catholic young wans are such crazy bitches you'd be better off not ta' have too many in the house at the one time. They might cut your bollocks off an' ate it, or somethin' just to spite the other one…… I suppose Mormon women are quieter than our headcases…..can ya get them ta' do any kinky stuff together for ya. Is it allowed like?"

Denny had, had enough. "I won't listen to any more, I have to go now, I'm very busy tonight."

He half ran out of the security hut to the van to get away and drove off at speed.

"See ya now Denny, be sure and call back for another chat soon. Nice little fella that. I must ask him more about them bleedin Mormons. Imagine Jimmy, two or three young wans at home gaggin' for it, d'ya think he'd be able for them. He'd have to ring you an' me ta' give 'um a hand. D'ya think he would Jimmy?"

"I'd say we'd be the first lads he'd call."

"Ha, ha Jimmy we'd give them a religious experience all right."

Poor old Denny was struggling from the get go. We were too rough, the job was too tough. We all liked him but I suppose we just wore him down, poor guy. After six months, he was swearing with the best of us, was starting to drink a bit, and generally was getting more like us lunatics every day. One night, after a year, mostly on nights in our delightful company, he told me he was quitting as, he thought he "might be losing his faith altogether."

"I thought I could cope Jimmy but I can't, yez have corrupted me."

The last said almost teary eyed. "Well Denny I'm sorry about that. We'll all be sorry to see ya go, you're a nice guy and we were glad to have you on board for a while."

"I know Jimmy and I'll miss youse too but I won't miss this fuckin' job. Ya have ta' see it from my point of view, I mean Jimmy I'm an ordained minister in a church. I can't deal with all this."

I understood only too well. "The road to hell was always paved with good intentions." I had left a few by the wayside myself. We all wished him well in his new career. The fellow who replaced him was a real dickhead but we had a way with dickheads and thankfully he did not last too long. I missed old Denny, a nice guy if there ever was.

Then there was 'Hedgehog', so called because his hair stuck out in all directions. Not overly endowed with brains, who thought the company and the bosses could do no wrong. I got on with the bosses well enough myself, but I was under no illusions, as to where we both stood. We had many a standoff and row. But we understood each other and knew where we were both coming from and while we were a bit wary of each other, we did not dislike each other.

But Hedgehog was a moron and when he wasn't ringing up the office telling tales, he was whinging about something or other they didn't care to hear. I found him quite hard to listen to for too long, as did Daisy the office secretary, whom he tormented on an ongoing basis, talking about all his woes, constantly. She was having an affair with the boss whose marriage had broken up. But she was always pleasant to deal with and was undoubtedly the most competent and diligent person in that office.

Hedgehog's parents had both died recently and while we were all sympathetic he began to get more and more erratic and difficult to deal with, starting rows for no reason with clients on contracts, showing up late, half in uniform, unshaven, unkempt, smelling a bit. A year had passed and he was getting worse, not better. His only company now, living in the house left by his parents, was his old dog Sherry.

One day Daisy rang me, after I had worked about a month of eighty-hour weeks without a day off. I was looking forward to my night off and I was looking forward to some rest. Daisy said, "I'm sorry

Jim but we're really badly stuck, could you come in tonight?"

In my sleep sodden haze I said okay. When I arrived, she rang me again to check that I was there and told me the reason I was in was that Hedgehog had rung in to say that his dog was ailing, was going to die that night and he was taking the night off.

I said, "Ya mean ta' tell me, I gave up my only night off for the last month for some bloody mutt. Daisy I'm not happy about this. Right now I'd gladly strangle Hedgehog and his stupid mutt." I mean I liked dogs myself but this was ridiculous. The dog didn't die that night or indeed for some time.

A friend of mine with a sicker sense of humour than me, found out the dog's name, got his address and sent a sympathy card with "Sherry RIP, any day now" written on it. Hedgehog didn't see the funny side of it and rang up Daisy blubbering and Daisy despite herself, thought it was hilarious and couldn't get off the phone quick enough, to laugh her head off.

Eventually Hedgehog started missing shifts and didn't show up for one reason or another. Too drunk, too lazy, who knows? So he was dismissed. One of the lads called to his house to see how he was, and found him sitting in the dark with another fellow who had also been sacked. They were now sharing the house. They had not paid the electricity bill so it had been cut off, no heat, no light, cupboards empty, no food. Just sitting there in the dark waiting for morning. They should never have left security work, at least they would be getting paid for that kind of thing.

I did not meet either fellow again. I did not particularly like either guy but it was hard not to feel sorry for them. "There but for the grace of God go I."

Chapter 21

A guard dog went missing in Finglas. Lo and behold, here came a bunch of kids leading it along. They saw it by the fence, felt sorry for it and decided to bring it for a walk. They returned it three hours later, much to our relief.

On another occasion a car park attendant had been on the beer all night, passing by the car park at 3am he realised he had forgotten to lock the car park. So he locked it up and went home. However, unknown to him a Garda patrol car had spotted the car park open and drove in to investigate. When they came back down to the gate, they were locked in. Benny the supervisor, doing his checks was most surprised to see the two irate Gardaí behind bars. "How did you get in?"

"Never you mind, just let us out right this minute."

Benny took his time. "I might not have the key."

He saw the fear on their faces, but of course he was only taking the piss and so finally he let them out. A week later, a row broke out at a fast food joint in town. A total free-for-all ensued involving chairs, tables, brush handles, knives and so on. The guard on duty reported it:

Guard: "There is a huge row after starting here. They're killing each other."

Benny: "I'm on my way, I'll call the police. Where are you?"

Guard: "I'm at the bus stop on me way home."

Benny: "Get back to your post."

Guard: "Not a chance, back to them psychos, no fuckin' way."

The row was sorted and the guard found another line of work.

Another fruitcake on duty in a major hospital, figured out how to access staff records on the computer. So he started ringing up the younger nurses at home trying to get them to go out with him on dates. The young ladies were quite scared at the amount of detail this weirdo seemed to know about them and it was some time before they actually figured out who it was and why he knew so much. It was all on file.

He got his marching orders. I was sitting with Danny one night in the car park and a sentimental song came on the radio about a father and son. "Ah," said Danny "that reminds me of me late father."

"Did you get on well with your Da, Danny?"

"No, I didn't, he was a total bollocks and I hated him. The best thing he ever did was to fuck off and die."

"Oh!"

Another fellow was on duty in a multinational mobile phone and computer supplier head office. When everyone was gone he used to switch a computer over so that he could play computer tennis on screen. Unfortunately being a bit drunk one night he made a mistake and managed to wipe £3 million worth of business off their files. Needless to say we got kicked out of there right quick.

Chapter 22

A few of the car park workers were starting to get headaches presumably from inhaling fumes in the badly ventilated underground car park, and a complaint was put in to some government work-safety department, who duly sent out someone. The hope was that there might be better ventilation provided and/or a bit more money for working in an unsafe environment.

The first I became aware of it was the box like gadget in the corner. "What's that thing for Danny?"

"It's for checkin the carbon monoxide and other car fumes, Jimmy, ta see if it's safe for us ta be workin here."

The boys wanted to be sure it worked so they made up a gadget with a big hose, one end of which was placed on the exhaust of one of their cars an hour or two before they went home, the other end was attached to the monitoring device, and the car was left with the engine running and revved up every now and again. This was done over a period of months and by the time it was collected there must have been as much lethal carbon monoxide pumped into the device as would kill a small army. The device was duly retrieved by the safety department and the car park workers waited with great interest to see the outcome of their selfless efforts."I'd say meself they'll havta close down this place and give us all a few paid days off while they upgrade this shitty ventilation system. D'ya not think so Jimmy," said Danny.

"You could be right Danny, but let's wait and see," I replied.

When the results came back it was the workers who were in for a shock. The car park management told the workers that the results were, that everything was fine and no need for any change at all. Everyone who knew the full story was in shock. "Rotten bunch of bastards, just like everything else in this country, someone got a few pound and say no more. Ya see what I tell ya Jimmy, ya can never win against these people. They have all the fuckin' money and all the power. The likes of us ordinary workin men don't count." Danny was not happy.

"You may well be right Danny, I'm sorry things didn't work out. It certainly makes you think."

It certainly did and I wondered how many other corrupt investigations had caused and would allow workers to die or suffer serious health problems in later life as a consequence of their actions or inactions as the case might be.

Christmas was now approaching, the troubles in Northern Ireland were in full swing, and attempts were made at some form of peace settlement without much success. People were getting killed on all sides, Protestants, Catholics, Security forces and of course members of the I.R.A and other nationalist and loyalist elements. There were also bombs going off in England. It was a complex, tense situation. The general opinion in Southern Ireland was that there was nothing to be done and that we were well out of it. "Let them murder each other till doomsday. No concern of ours."

Unfortunately loyalists in the North decided it might be our concern and they made threats to start a major bombing campaign in Dublin as a Christmas present to all of our Christmas shoppers. So we were put on the alert in the car parks of the city centre and had to stop cars coming in and make drivers open their boots so that we could ogle through whatever they might have therein.

A couple of bombs were sent down on the Dublin to Belfast trains, with timers set to go off when they reached Dublin – they were found before they could go off. A Special Branch Detective was sent in to us to give us a lecture on what to look for; how to check under cars, how to spot suspect packages and other riveting stuff like that.

We were quietly shitting a brick. I mean what could we do if some psycho loyalist terrorist came to town hell bent on reducing the population of Dublin? We were unarmed. What in God's name could we do if we found something? Perhaps we could talk them to death. Joking, we suggested various approaches among ourselves, "I suppose sir ya hardly have a bit of 'oul semtex or any hand grenades in your 'oul car or about you anywhere?"

Reply: "Begod now ya have me there. What d'ya know? I have a truck full of explosives. Imagine that? I just wanted to see would yez notice anything. Sure if ya give us a hand I can empty it out. Leave it with you and collect it when I'm going home."

"Ah sure that be just grand sir, have a nice day now."

People from the North said to us, when we apologised for the inconvenience, that they felt a bit safer that we were doing this, as they were quite used to it. It was more than we felt; this was no fun at all.

But Christmas passed uneventfully enough. Someone found a shotgun in a fellow's car trunk and Gardaí were notified but it turned out it was a legally held, fully licensed gun and the man was allowed to proceed on his way. Harmless enough I suppose, but it did beg the question: what was he doing with a shotgun in his car in the heart of Dublin city? A bit of duck shooting in Stephens Green perhaps.

Anyhow the panic ended after Christmas and we all breathed a collective sigh of relief. Got a bit of sleep and spent some of our hard earned overtime money. In other words, we all got as drunk as monkeys the first chance we got.

Chapter 23

Danny the car park worker went missing for a couple of days. We all thought he was just on a bender, no big deal. But when he got back, the story he told me, explaining his absence was certainly different.

On his day off he did as we correctly assumed- go "on the beer" with a friend of his. Now after the first pub, he and his friend said they would both drive to "town" (the city centre) separately. However Danny decided on his way, to overtake some driver, a driver going too slow in Danny's opinion. So he overtook him. So far, so good.

However, the other driver was not best pleased and the first chance he got, he overtook Danny. Danny decided to 'show him' and overtook him again. The other fellow reciprocated and the race was on with horns blaring, tempers flaring, two fingered hand gestures and so on. After overtaking his man again, Danny got stuck at traffic lights, out jumps the man from the car behind him and raced up to Danny's car. Danny used to box as a youngster and had a devilish temper. Out jumped Danny "Pow," Danny knocked him out cold and left him lying on the ground at the lights and drove away.

He got to the nightclub where he was to meet his friend but there was no sign of him. He joined the queue. A few minutes later the doorman walked down the queue behind him and Danny heard him say, "No way, no way, ya' won't be getting' in."

"But why not?," said a familiar voice.

"No way, no way......"

Danny looked around and there was his friend, drunker than before, queuing with his arm around a young traveller girl he found begging on the side of the road, complete with one of those tartan blankets they used to wrap around themselves to keep warm, when they were begging at that time.

Danny kept low and eventually got into the nightclub and even managed to get a woman to bring him home with her (of course his wife would have cut his balls off if she knew). After the nightclub he went back to her place and had his bit of fun and away home to wifey. However, as he was rather drunk and rather tired and was, to say the least, driving quite erratically. A Garda pulled him over and breathalysed him. It went off the scale. He was duly arrested and brought to the station. He was hoping they might be lenient on him until he spotted a familiar face with a swollen jaw. It was the 'road rage' fellow and it seems he was a plain clothes detective and he worked in that particular station. He eyed Danny with cold, hard eyes as he walked by.

"So ya' see Jimmy. I spent the night in jail, all the next day in court and got £1,000 of a fine for me trouble," Danny concluded. "At least the guards didn't give me a kickin', I thought they would. I suppose I was lucky."

"Danny, you're one mad fuckin' lunatic." All I could do was laugh my head off.

Soon Danny was laughing too. "You're a bollocks Jimmy, no sympathy at all for anyone." But I laughed all the more and so did he with tears running down our faces.

We were doing security on an office block adjacent to Baggot St. in the South city. The road out front was where the "ladies of the night" operated. Yes, it was a well known red light zone. The ladies were doing a roaring trade with cars around the block, late into the night. It was a bit like the Grand Prix, all vying to get the ladies into their cars. There were Mercedes, Jaguars, BMW's vying with beat up rust buckets and to say the least, less fashionable vehicles. Into this mix came the local vice squad, who when they weren't looking for freebies themselves, hassled both working girl and client alike and from time to time prosecuted a few when the humour took them. It was of great interest to us watching the action as it played out. We could go up high enough in the building to get a good view of the proceedings. There was a drunk who walked up to one of the girls and grabbed her behind. I don't know what she had in her bag, but when she hit him with it, he went down and stayed down for some time. There were fights among the girls themselves over whose "patch" it was and who could use that part of the road. There was a three car collision at the junction, well two cars and a van to be precise. Obviously, with all the young ladies in short skirts lining the road, it is indeed possible they were a bit distracted. One young lady was wearing a fur coat and when she was approaching a car she would let it swing open, revealing she had only her underwear on, no wonder cars were crashing. I had my own dog with me once at work as I did not live too far away, he was company for me. I was patrolling the car park in the dark and as I was coming round to the front there was a small, pretty, young lady in a micro mini skirt, waiting for a client to approach, at the bus stop with her back to me. Unfortunately my dog, a large collie mongrel was a bit overfriendly and promptly trotted up to her and shoved his cold nose straight up between her legs from behind. Such an ear piercing shriek she let out frightened the life out of me. The dog didn't seem too bothered and just frisked about in a manner that said, 'Now wasn't that a great laugh? Amn't I a great doggie for doin' that?' He repeatedly tried to stick his nose back in the same place.

I said, "I'm sorry about that."

She said, "Jaysus I didn't know what the hell was that bleedin' cold thing. I'll wear me bleedin' knickers in future."

I was trying hard not to laugh, leashing the dog. I knew she was still shaking. I apologised again and went back into the building where I laughed my head off.

I never did see the big deal about prostitution in society; they wanted money, clients wanted nookie, what was the problem? As long as everyone's rights were protected and nobody was exploited against their wishes, I thought it was a useful service to all. It was really just the location of such zones that created the problem. I mean no one wanted one on their doorstep. But at the same time when they started to operate in the car park of the building I was guarding I had to intervene.

It took a while for me to notice the occasional car and pedestrians trotting in and out unseen, until I happened on a couple in action at the back wall. I arrived as they were finishing. The client departed and when she had settled herself, she walked over and handed me some money.

I said, "What's that for?" she replied, "I'll do the same deal with you as with your mate Pat, a tenner a head."

I was certainly not adverse to taking easy money or turning a blind eye when no one was harmed by it. But it would only be a question of time before the Gardaí followed one of the good ladies into the car park and questions would be asked. Also, I lived locally and preferred a quiet life. "Whatever deal is between you and Pat, is between you and Pat, none of my concern but ya' can't be at that, when I'm on duty. If you were caught I'd be sacked. I'm sorry an' all but no way. Here's your money back, thanks all the same. Good luck to ya'."

"Fair enough," she replied, you're a nice lad yourself, would like an 'oul go wit me."

"No, no thanks, thanks, good luck now." I ushered her out, went back in the building and breathed a sigh of relief. I was relieved she hadn't turned nasty as I had seen some of them do, watching from the window. Mostly after that, things were fairly quiet and I even managed to catch up on some sleep.

Pat seemed to have plenty of money for a time, until one day I saw him with two black eyes and his face looked like someone had been doing a dance on his head.Perhaps a pimp had thought he was moving in on his action. He wouldn't tell me what happened. But his high living seemed to end shortly after that.

Peace once again.

Chapter 24

Winter was closing in, I was sick of the nights, sick of the crap that went with the job. I was on my own again, on a building site which would become a major shopping complex years later, indeed the biggest in Europe. I was tired, I needed sleep. I had just broken up with my latest girlfriend, I was not a happy camper. I had no car at the time and it took me three buses and two hours of travelling to get on site. Furthermore the foreman was a dickhead and if you were five minutes late you got a verbal roasting. I was on for sixteen hours that night and I was hoping to get some sleep.

There was a major illegal halting site for travellers across the road, with a few hundred travellers therein and they just would not let us alone. If it wasn't the kids, it was the grown-ups. We were in a Porta-Cabin with metal grills on the windows and it had become a game among the children to watch us all night as we were easy to see with the lights on, and every time we nodded off they would hop a stone off one of the grills of the Porta-Cabin. There were plenty of things to steal on the site and they did not like us one bit, as we were coming between them and a bit of lucrative larceny. Try as I might, they just would not let me sleep, even the poor guard dog was nervous. Every time my head dropped "bang" a stone hopped off the grill. Our personal relationship with the travellers was at an all-time low, so there was not much point trying to appeal to their better nature.

Recently on one occasion, one of our lads- an ex army chap- tired and overworked like myself, was obliging a number of travellers on horses by opening a locked gate to let them out yet again, from a place they should not have been in, in the first place. He went to the gate holding the guard dog who was barking and lunging. Unfortunately, a couple of travellers thought it might be a bit of a lark to threaten him and give him a bit if abuse while he was unlocking the gate. If they had known Iggy as I did, they would have remained polite to the end. Iggy was not particularly big, normally good natured, afraid of very little. Under normal circumstances he was very easy to deal with but when he lost it, he knew no boundaries and he became a stone cold psycho. I had heard he had been jumped on by a gang of thugs on his way home one night. He almost killed a couple of them; injured most of them and even bit a lump of flesh out of one fellows arm. They fled, leaving one of their number on the ground with a cracked skull and dragging another between them. Iggy even went back on a number of subsequent nights with an iron bar and made serious efforts to find them again intent on finishing what he started. He never did find them, lucky them! So this abuse, at this moment was indeed ill advised. He had, also that evening, had a major row with his wife and one of the travellers said something like, "Ya little bollocks you're lucky we don't kick the shite out of you."

Iggy stopped unlocking the gate "What did you say?"

"I said you're lucky we don't kick the shite out of you."

Iggy's eyes bulged.

"You fuckin' knacker, scumbag, bastard, do you think I'm here to take shit from low life sacks of shit like yourselves?"

So saying, he unleashed the mad guard dog and set him on the horses, who bolted with riders in tow. He managed to yank the biggest man off his horse before he got away and proceeded to thump the living life out of him and after opening the gate and disposing of the now prone traveller he ran to a shed in the compound, found a large can of petrol and a pick handle and went over to the halting site; stood on a small hill and began to roar, "If I get anymore shit from you fuckheads I'll burn every caravan in this shithole to ashes; see if I don't."

He left with complete silence around him. Needless to say they left Iggy alone after that. Some of the young men on the horses had wound up miles away, some in ditches, some in bushes and briars, others landed in water. No indeed, Iggy was not one to be trifled with. The funny thing was, he didn't particularly dislike travellers, it was mostly the timing of their abuse and the fact was that he would take crap from nobody. He got left alone from then on, but the rest of us were not so lucky. One fellow officer who lived locally and used to come to work on a bicycle had got into a verbal altercation with a big traveller. The traveller tried to knock him off his bike with his van. Frankie took to carrying a hatchet in his work bag, going in and out to work.

I was tired and hoping for a quiet night. Some chance, suddenly there was an almighty, flash which lit up the whole sky and then all lights went out, street lights , houses, shops in the major town three miles away. It looked like the whole of Dublin city was suddenly in darkness. I managed to find a torch which wasn't great but it was something. I radioed in to report what had happened and went out with the dog to look around. All seemed quiet but how dark it was. I jumped when a voice spoke to me along the fence. It was an old lady traveller, "If you want to come over later young lad, for a cup of tay I'll bile the kittle on the gas if you've no way of bilin' the kittle."

"Thanks very much," I said but declined not fancying my chances of making it back alive or that anything would be left on the site when I got back. But it was nice of her to offer. She said a couple of youngsters from the camp had been messing about and hurled an iron bar onto the power lines which blew the lot, and put out the power to a few hundred thousand homes in the process. Even the Garda Station was in darkness. That night was one long, cold miserable night, with no heater, no kettle, to make tea, no light to read a book, even the guard dog looked miserable. To top it all, the workers were late arriving next morning and I had to wait an hour just to catch the first of my three buses home. When the security office opened I rang up and said, "If I am ever put on that contract again, I'll quit."

The bosses brought me into the office to give me shit and test my resolve but I was not for turning and fully intended to quit, if forced to go back. Thankfully I was not asked to go again.

Chapter 25

One of those complicated stories I have often tried to put to paper, was the story of Alphie. Another ex navy man, a big lump of a fellow from Dublin city. He had a peculiar misshapen big head with curly hair that stuck out everywhere. He was a likeable fellow, always cheery, always broke and always looking to borrow. Slightly alcoholic, (what's new?) and generally not the worst but what a bull-shitter he was. He told lies and tall tales as no one else could. His conversation would often depart from the road of reality into whatever fantasy zone he happened to be in. He thought he was an ex commando, next he might say he was gun runner with a contract out on someone he didn't like. He couldn't decide if he was related to royalty or an axe murderer.

One day he would say he was a pimp with a string of foreign women on his payroll. The next, he was an ex parish priest who had worked in the Vatican. He and another fellow, his friend, were always broke and looking for "The Lend" of money which was never seen again. Sometimes they would steal money from the tills in the car parks, much to the consternation of the attendants who preferred to do their own stealing. I was working on the docks with him one day and he was talking about hiring a hit man. Then he said, "Ya see that fellow on that ship?"

"Yes"

"I'd say you could shoot him dead from here if you had a good crossbow. What do ya think?"

"I never really gave it much thought."

"Well I'd say meself you could, if the wind wasn't too strong"

"Fair enough"

"Jimmy"

"Yes"

"Have you any money on ya?"

"Not much."

"Any chance of a lend?"

"No."

"Fair enough... Yeah I'd say you'd definitely kill him if ya had a good crossbow..."

Danny from the car parks, was giving him a lift home one night after dark. Danny was a likeable family man, a bit of an alcoholic who had once been a criminal, and knew some extremely dangerous people.

Alphie: Thanks for the lift Danny.

Danny: No problem.

Alfie: Where would I hire a hit man for a £1000?

Danny: Stop talking shite.

Alfie: Danny?

Danny: Yes

Alphie: Any chance of a lend?

Danny: No.

Alphie: Fair enough... Danny?

Danny: Yes Alphie.

Alphie: Would you sell your wife and kids for a million pounds?

Danny: Alphie get the fuck out of my car, ya fuckin' mental case, I won't listen to one more word of your oul shite. Get out before I kill ya, ya dopey bollocks.

Sensibly Alfie got out and made his own way home that day and made sure he kept his mouth shut on the rare occasion that Danny ever did give him a lift again.

Sometime later I was talking to Benny from Belfast.

I said to Benny "I'll tell ya Benny, Alphie has really lost the plot lately."

"How do you mean Jimmy?"

"The bullshit he comes out with lately comes straight from the Mother Goose."

"It's funny you should say that, he told me the other day some fellow offered him a half a million to go out and kill blacks in South Africa..."

Now here is where Alphie's story crosses the line and leaves the road of reality itself. If you don't believe this neither would I, especially if it came from Alphie, but it didn't. Well, Alphie and his friend got sacked for stealing money from the car park tills. One night sometime later, Danny was on duty in the cash box,, when a furtive figure went by, trying not to be noticed. "Alphie is that you?"

"Yeah , how ya Danny?"

"You don't look so good Alphie are you sick?"

"I'm a bit scared Danny, I came here to rob ya. I need money in a bad way, I'm in deep shit."

"What's wrong?"

"I got some drugs from some heavy people and I never paid them back and they're goin' to break me legs Danny, so will you let me rob ya?"

"No way Alphie, I can't we're watched too closely now, I'd be sacked.

Alfie started to blubber... "These fellas are psychos, they'll fuckin kill me. I'm trying to get money to get out of the country. I'm not lyin." Tears poured down his face. He took out a massive knife, a blue balaclava and an old jacket he would wear for the robbery and discard afterwards, putting back on his good leather jacket. He looked shaky and unwell and not fit for much. Eventually, he said, "I havta have the money, d'ya know any car parks around here I could rob?"

Danny: There is one down the road if you want to give it a try.

Alfie: Where is it?

Danny: Down near Crawford Street beside Castle Lane"

Alfie: Yeah, I think I know that one... Right I'll see ya Danny.
Danny: See ya.

Half an hour later Alfie is back, red faced and sweating, shaking like a leaf.

Danny: What happened"?
Alfie: I left me good jacket on the wall near the car park. I put on me old spare jacket, I put on me balaclava and took out me knife. There was only an oul fella in the cash box. I ran at him with the knife and roared" 'Give me the fuckin money' and he was givin it to me an all and then this big fit lookin fucker came outta nowhere roarin at me and I legged it and left me good jacket on the wall.
Danny: What'll ya do now?
Alfie: I don't know Danny, I'm fucked." Putting his head into his hands he started to cry.
Alfie: Danny, please let me rob ya?
Danny: If you say it again Alfie I'll break your legs!
Alfie: Fair enough Danny... Danny?
Danny: Yes Alfie.
Alfie: Any chance of a lend?
Danny: Here's a fiver, and if ya annoy me again I'll burst ya with a box.
Alfie: Thanks Danny, I'll see ya so.
Danny: See ya.

Sometime later, there was a ship on the river Liffey which collided with another ship in thick fog and went down with many casualties. It stated in the newspaper that the person who first raised the alarm on board the ship was "Alfie Maguire," who also went down with the ship. The ship was found to be smuggling contraband in various forms, including drugs and guns. His fantasy had become a reality.

Myself and Danny were talking about it many months later:

Danny: I think it was the sort of way Alfie would have liked to go don't ya think Jimmy?

Jimmy: Yes, I think he would have, poor old Alfie.

Danny: Poor old Alfie.

Chapter 26

It was Christmas time again. We all knew that over the Christmas we would all be working round the clock. No socialising, just work and plenty of it. It was indeed a rare occasion that we would all be off on the same night, as usually most would be on duty. However, a few weeks before Christmas, a night came that enough of us were off for a good drinking session, better known as "a good piss up" - the nearest we were going to get to a Christmas party. So the night came and we hit the town hard. We started in one pub and went to another and another and another. Now there might have been another but I'm just not too sure as after the second pub, conscious thought had become decidedly difficult. Anyhow, at some stage we felt a night club was called for to round off the night and we all headed for the one decided on.

Our route took us past our beloved seat of government, Dail Eireann. There was an open area just beside The Dail and a few lads decided to have a "Piss" (alright then, urinate if one must be polite). I was absolutely bursting so I decided to release the pressure also. Lo and behold along came a couple of "Rookie" Gardaí, on this most heinous crime scene, this insult to our great seat of democracy, the building in which those saintly paragons of virtue presided over our beloved and saintly country. I looked over my shoulder and said "Fuck it" to myself and continued to urinate. The rest of the lads had their willies in like a shot and were all grovelling and apologetic. I was never much for the grovelling especially to authority. So I was nicked. I was asked for my name and address. Unfortunately, in my inebriated state of mind it seemed like a good idea to give a false name and address, under the notion that any sort of criminal record even for urinating on the public highway would impede future employment in the security industry, with other prospective employers, as most of them did check these things. I had not figured on them getting on the radio and checking it out and finding this fellow did not exist. Now drunken people are not commonly noted for making wise decisions and foolishly enough at this point I decided to come clean and even produced ID. Well this young guard much shorter than me went into overdrive. He was already red in the face at my indifference to him, he now became apoplectic, his eyes almost coming out of their sockets. "Right" he said "That's it, I'm arresting you."

"Jumped up arrogant little bollocks!" I thought, to myself mind you.

He recited some old shite to me, one of them radioed for the police van, lo and behold it arrived in no time at all and a heap of cops came from various locations, some with batons drawn, hoping to give someone a good beating. I braced myself for what was to come, I had never been arrested before and I didn't like it one bit. In fact it coloured my thinking about Gardaí even to this day. "Nice to think my tax money is being well spent" I thought as I stepped into the van.

I smiled and laughed and joked about it but I really didn't find it all that funny. Well I didn't get a beating, one small Mercy. Down to Pearse St. Garda Station I was brought. My details were taken, my pockets were emptied and my shoe laces were taken off me and I was put into a skanky looking smelly shithole of a cell reminiscent of a scene from H-Block during the "Dirty Protest" i.e. shit smeared on the walls. They slammed the big prison door behind me and turned off the light. I was bursting for a wee again but wasn't going to give them the satisfaction of banging on the door. There was a toilet at the end of the bunk, which accounted for some of the smell but I didn't know it was there in the darkness. I lay down in the darkness on the ratty old bunk and pulled the grey smelly old prison blanket over me. It reeked of disinfectant, I wondered why? I contrived to sleep but I could not. I heard the little peephole shutter sliding back as a guard peeped in at me, to see what I was doing. I heard them whispering, "What's he doing now?"

"He's asleep under that smelly old blanket"

"Hee hee hee........"

There was a quiet impotent rage burning within me. The more so because I had worked all year in my nowhere job locked away from people guarding property with no social life, now living alone in a house I had bought. On a rare night I had a chance to socialize, here I was locked up again. "Fuck it" I thought "Try and sleep."

I lay on the bunk in the total blackness and stewed for about three hours. Suddenly the door was unbolted. "Right," said the guard. "Get your stuff, ya can go."

A friend of mine was waiting outside, the rest had fled. He had found out which station I had been brought to and had remained outside annoying the police offering to put money in the police "Charity box" or whatever they might suggest, trying to persuade them to let me out. Eventually, I presume they got sick of both of us, I wasn't entertaining enough and he wouldn't leave. Out I came and I got my stuff. "Here sign this" I signed.

"What happens next?" I asked.

"I wouldn't think you will hear any more about it," said a more decent guard "Good luck now and safe home."

And away we went, my friend and I, but the night was over, it was too late to go anywhere now. We headed back to my place, talked shit for a while, had a beer each. I showed him the spare room and went to bed myself. The next few weeks were strange; everybody in the firm rang me, or contacted me in some way, even people in the firm I had not spoken to in years. From the bosses to the office secretary, to the lowest officer, I mean everyone. No one mentioned my arrest, but the pretexts they rang me on, were pretty thin and I noticed how they all gradually steered me round to the subject they wanted to hear about with the well worn "Well anything strange lately?" Even over the phone I could hear the suppressed laughter. This was the best laugh they had in years and they milked it for all it was worth. I find it funny now, but at the time I was not amused. Still I did not deprive them and told the tale sparing no detail. They went away satisfied. I was now a hero it seemed.

A friend of mine who joined the firm a few years after me said, "Ya know – I was dying to meet you even before we did meet. You were almost like a legend. Everyone has a different "Jim Linnane story." You were my hero even before we met."

This last sentence I assure you was tongue in cheek but I shuddered to think what he had heard. In fairness in those days I was a bit of a lunatic and not everything that happened has been committed to paper, understandably. It wasn't that I actively sought out mad cap situations, but in fairness, I constantly seemed to wind up in them mind you, my "comrades in arms" assisted me greatly to this end.

Chapter 27

In a job where you were often dealing with the public, you really never knew what to expect. A young fellow in a car park was on duty at the foot of the "in" ramp, keeping pedestrians from walking up where cars were coming down. A poor young man who had decided to kill himself, jumped off the top floor of the car park and landed in front of the horrified guard on the ramp. "He opened up just like a tin of beans" he told Benny later.

I said to Benny to watch the young fellow who saw this. "He seemed to be calm enough," said Benny. "I thought he would be worse."

Now, I'm no psychiatrist, but all I said was "Wait and see."

Sure enough, about a week later young Martin, for no reason, started ranting on the radio, making no sense, reading passages from the bible and crying and so on. I think he eventually went for counselling.

Another time I was on duty in a cement and block making factory and one of our young fellows started shouting on the radio. I ran out in time to see a ball of flame coming up from the far end of the yard behind the blocks where the young fellow was. "I'm being petrol bombed," and he was!

I grabbed a steel pipe and ran across the yard. As I came around a pile of blocks, they threw another one. But it bounced harmlessly and just burned some grass on the hill where they were standing just above us. There were four of them, the same four who had beaten up a guard, stolen a radio, stolen cars and burned them and had broken into a number of offices in that compound. They were implicated in one stabbing. However, they were minors and the police didn't even bother trying to arrest them. So here I was, with my steel pipe, running towards them. The great bank of earth had been bulldozed there by the company, to create a high bank to keep out thieves, like them, but it proved ideal for them to launch missiles down on our heads. "Fuck it," I thought. I ran on, all they had left was an empty bottle and they threw it. It smashed on the blocks beside my face and a piece of glass struck me on the cheek but I was okay. I ran up the embankment swinging the pipe and they ran, just as well for me too. I chased them for a bit but they were too fast. I went back to Pete to find he was alright, just a bit shaken. Two more of our lads came up from the quarry and the front gate and rambled around with us just to show numbers and discourage any further onslaughts. It was quiet for the rest of the day which was a Sunday, as I recall.

Another occasion, another contract a friend of mine, Dillon, was in the coal yard and a craving for alcohol took over. The site was very isolated; he had no car with him today, another Sunday. He looked in a forty-foot coal lorry and sure enough, he found keys. He opened the main gate and drove it straight to the local village; put on his hazard lights, in Main Street, blocking the whole street. He skipped in to the off license, got a case of beer, put it in the lorry and drove back to the yard. Though he had never driven a lorry before, he told me, "those moron lorry drivers can do it, how hard can it be?"

One day, again Sunday, he was on duty in Dublin City, bored mindless and craving alcohol. I was off duty and he was on. I phoned him.

"Jimmy, I'm in a bad way. I'm stuck here; I've no money and no beer. Ya' know me, I'll be gone off me rocker by evening."

I said I had some beer in the fridge and I'd drop them in. "Oh, would ya? I won't forget this Jimmy, ya' always bail me out. You're a great pal."

I was in sympathy with all who bore the hardships of the long hours and tedium, so I understood well his dilemma.

He let me in when I got there. We sat down and had a few beers, talked a lot of crap; the usual. Then we played baseball with the empty cans, as the beer kicked in. One would throw and the other would bat with half a brush handle. Whacking them off neon signs in the building and plate glass windows in the closed down take away.

"Ya know Jimmy, I owe you one. I'm goin ta' bring you on the beer with me." I knew he had no money. He went to the toilets downstairs but didn't come back up. Eventually I went downstairs and sure enough he had almost forced open the cash drawer of the pay phone. He had done, and was doing such damage to the payphone in the process, that when I could not discourage him, I simply helped him to finish the job with less damage to the appliance. When the change was counted there was about £60. Not a bad sum back then. We spent the rest of the day in the pub across the road. When his relief, Harry, arrived we both staggered over to greet him. Harry took in the scene at once, "Fair play to ye lads, I'll say nothin'."

We neglected to mention the payphone. We had a chat, said our goodbyes and off to another pub with music this time. Dillon had a girlfriend at that time and I had not, so clearly he wanted to finish his session at home and away he went. I was staggering back and decided to get one of them new fire extinguishers off the wall in the building we were minding. "Is there anything else you want while you're at it Jim, a few plates or one of them fancy dispensers?"

"No, not a bit Harry. Thanks all the same." So home I staggered, three miles with a fire extinguisher on shoulder. Alright, I admit it; I was just as much of a screwball as any of them. But it couldn't be helped, life was for living. Amen.

Chapter 28

In a well known North Dublin shopping centre the lads were getting bored, with state of the art C.C.T.V. Looking around the shopping centre was not much excitement, so they removed the clip which limited the various cameras rotations. Now they could turn 360°. "Now you're talkin." So they started to scan all the local houses for any curtains open and any sexy action and when they did, they zoomed in tight, really tight and recorded it, every detail.

There was even a young couple who used to have a shag every Friday night in a phone box at 3am- every detail on film. The next night when things got quiet, the lads would sit around, watch the footage recorded previously and make comments about the action.

"Look at the arse on her."

"Begod, I'd say she's enjoyin' that."

"He's fairly roddin' her."

"She's a fair goer for an oul' wan."

"I'd say that young wan' has a tight fanny. Nice tits too." And so on.

It was by accident that a supervisor happened to flick through the footage of wall to wall amateur porn, albeit with unwitting participants. There was hell to pay. Threats of dismissals, suspensions, legal action and the like. But it came to nought. The cameras were scrupulously checked from then on. No more naughty business after that.

At one point a new security firm replaced us in a shopping centre. It transpired that they were an even bigger shower of lunatics than us. There were a number of episodes. I was told about, by a friend who worked for them. One was an old boy who thought he was clever switching off the camera so that he could go down onto the main floor to load up his car, which he did, with anything he fancied. It was night time and the other guard was on patrol in the grounds. It transpired that the camera had been off and he had inadvertently switched them on, to record no less, and of course when the footage got checked, bye, bye old chap.

Another fellow acquired a stun gun, which, for those who don't know is a 'glorified battery' about the size of a security radio. It has a couple of terminals on the end of it which, when touched to someone or something and the button is pressed, will deliver a jolt of electricity – enough to floor a cart horse and possibly kill anyone with a weak heart. Sunday as usual being the preferred day of mischief; two of their guys and one of ours who was on duty next door, got together for a chat. The stun gun was produced and examined by all. "Very impressive!." "Did you ever try it out?"

"No, not yet."

They each looked at each other but no one volunteered. "I will in my bollocks, you try it."

No one did, but then three sets of eyes focused on the poor unsuspecting Doberman walking in front of them, on a lead. I was told the poor thing splayed out on the ground like a cat run over by a steam roller. When he came around, the doggie was not too happy and showed every sign of attacking all three men. Somehow, they got him back in his cage and left him there after that. So much for the experiment.

Of course, it was only a matter of time before some idiot used it on a person. During a fairly minor row, a teenager got a bit physical with one of the guards. They dragged him over by the fence and "Bam!" Stun gun. For a few minutes they thought he was dead and were a bit worried. But when he survived they thought it was all a good laugh but the victim didn't, and thereafter the gloves were off. Other more dangerous people got involved. A dog was found with a crossbow bolt through his heart, still in his cage. Guards started to be set upon more regularly and one or two got serious beatings.

Another fellow who foiled a couple of minor robberies was targeted and they called to his house. Not finding him home, they beat up his wife and son and left the message that they would get him eventually. They trashed the house and left. Soon thereafter the firm had to be taken out of there for their own sake.

Chapter 29

Another chap in our firm who was a bit of a moron but, I suppose he wasn't the worst, had a knack for stirring things up. Seemed to think, like so many, that wearing a uniform entitled him to do and say what he liked. Once he confided in a fellow worker, that he and his wife liked "kinky sex," nothing wrong with that. But he said he liked to pour lots of cream over her and then have sex in the mess. Foolishly, someone told me and my big mouth being what it was, I told others, ending the tale with the obvious quip, "that marriage will soon go sour." But that's not the reason I thought he was a moron. It rained savagely one day and a couple of passing youngsters from the local tenements had ducked in under the front canopy for a bit of shelter till it passed outside a city centre car park.

"Oi!" said Brian, "Hop it!"

"What did you say?" came the reply.

"Come on, out of there."

"But it's lashing rain, we'll go when it's over."

"Listen, if you don't move your arses I'll have to get physical and teach you both a bit of manners." So they went, but, when the rain stopped they came back, but they were not alone. I do not know if you ever saw 'Zulu Dawn', the film. However, if you could envision a Dublin version of that film, comprised mostly of ten to fourteen year olds, carrying sticks, bricks, broken bottles, knives, steel bars and other stuff along those lines. Brian locked himself in the toilet and quietly shit himself. They would have beaten him to a pulp was it not for the car park attendant who knew some of their fathers and possibly saved his life. Another trick of Brian's was grabbing young underage girls from the tenements, caught taking a short cut through the car park and under the pretext of throwing them out, would drag them into a quiet corner and start feeling them up. Talk about playing with fire. I found out early on, what a complete coward he was. While on duty on a building site with him, there was a break in. When we became aware that they were on the premises, he just went to pieces, shaking violently and blubbering like a baby. I asked him to radio the supervisor but he couldn't do that. I had to struggle with him to get the radio off him to call it in and then I had to grab a baton and a dog and go out to deal with it on my own, but they had seen our antics and were gone back over the fence. When I came back he had locked himself in an office and only came out when Benny arrived. We looked around outside, in daylight and found some of what had been stolen, roofing felt, tools, lead and stuff like that, hidden in the grass at the back. So the night was not a total loss. More than I could say for Brian.

Of course I had my own share of mishaps. In the cement factory a stone throwing match developed between us and some youths, up on the bank. There was no particular malice between us and these kids; it was just really a bit of tomfoolery. A young fellow I knew threw a stone at me and got me in the leg, it hurt a lot, but I thought nothing of it. My work boot felt wet and I looked down. It looked just like someone had thrown a can of red paint on my boot and my trouser leg. I lifted up my trouser leg and copious quantities of blood were gushing from a varicose vein in my leg, which had burst.

I told the lads what had happened on the radio, and a couple of them came flying up in a car, driving as if they were under sniper fire in Beirut. "Get in, get in." I was helped in.

"It's not that bad lads, I'm not on the critical list or anything" but they were having none of it, I was rushed to the main gate and an ambulance was called. A fellow, I did not particularly like, produced a first aid kit; his hour had come. He had done a first aid course once and now was his chance to shine. He bandaged up my leg. The reason I did not like him was because he loved ringing up the boss and getting people in trouble: telling tales, which occasionally got people sacked needlessly. So the ambulance came and I was carted off. The hospital was crammed with people and after waiting two hours and expecting to wait another three, I said "To hell with this." I signed myself out to go home. As luck would have it a supervisor arrived at the hospital to see how I was and brought me back to the factory to get my car. I went home; my shift was over anyhow. Mr. First Aid told everyone it was "touch and go" for a while and that I "nearly didn't make it" and I probably wouldn't have if it wasn't for his intervention. "What a twat!" I thought.

Chapter 30

While on duty in a well known set of offices on the south side of Dublin, the water to the toilets had been off for some time and the toilets were still being used by us all. The smell was getting awful. So I looked in the workshop for something to kill the smell. I found a tin of something that smelled awful too, to drown the other smell. It helped a bit but there were still little flies hovering in the bowl. I thought "I wonder if it's flammable, if it burned it might clear out those little flies."

I procured a match and threw it in. "Kaboom!" I don't know what it was but boy was it flammable! A flame shot off the toilet and blackened the ceiling. "Holy Shit!"

I ran around like a headless chicken, looking for water or something to beat it or put it out. I whacked it with a newspaper, it caught fire. It was burning very strongly now, "Holy Shit! Please God don't let this whole place burn down. Please, please, please... What will I do?"

If I threw water on it, would it make it worse? I was in such a panic. I more or less did nothing, well nothing constructive anyway. Then something strange happened. The heat was so intense the toilet bowl split at the bottom. "Oh no, it's going to spread all over the floor. Oh shit, I'm so fired! but as the liquid poured out of the broken toilet the flames started to hiss and fizzle out.

"Alleluia, it's a miracle! Thank you Jesus...Thank you, thank you, thank you...I'll be ever so good from now on....well, at least for this week....oh, thank you..."

A month later my boss was in looking around. "Look at this Jim, they even broke the toilet bowl, they're just like pigs."

"Yes, Ron. You're so right, they're just like pigs....it's just a disgrace." If he only knew the half of it.

Some youths stole a dumper from the building site in Finglas. About ten youths were on board, tearing down the carriage way through the traffic. It was day-time. Workers and security guards – we all crammed into the foreman's car and he set off in pursuit. They had a head start, but dumpers are not known for speed. However, their advantage was they could drive over or through almost anything. So when we were catching up they just drove over the carriageway divide and headed in the opposite direction, leaving us stuck in the traffic, trying hard to turn around. They drove up an embankment and headed for the local football pitch. After a two mile detour we got there too. We cornered them near a low wall and we all jumped out and charged the dumper. The youths knew the game was up, so they jumped the wall and ran away. One of the workers drove the dumper back with a guard riding "shotgun" in case he got attacked. He didn't.

It was Halloween, one supervisor who was the very devil when it came to sneaking up on us, trying to catch us asleep; which we often were, got hold of an "old man" mask from one of the lads. You know those rubber masks that looked so real. McKenna was such a son-of-bitch we almost admired him, but not quite. So he arrived at a creepy old house in West Dublin at about 4am; rolling up with his lights off, his sneaking up tactics, worthy of a commando unit. There was a window to a room where we were based in, high up on the side of the building. McKenna got a ladder from the store room at the side and put it up to the window. He climbed up and took a peak.

Of course the man was asleep in a comfy chair. McKenna donned the mask, up again. He pressed his face up to the window and began to hammer on the glass and roar for all he was worth. The man woke up, saw the apparition, which seemed to be floating in mid air and began to scream with fright. He and the chair tumbled over backwards. He dived into a corner shaking and gibbering and even pissed his pants. He cowered and screamed until McKenna took off the mask, delighted with the result.

"I might have had a heart attack you bastard." True enough.

"You shouldn't have been asleep. You're not paid to sleep." Also true, but still and all, as with all things in life you can go too far. McKenna did eventually get the boot, I suppose I might have helped him on his way. I used to like him once but he went from being funny to just plain nasty. The fellow who got the fright quit the following week. He was a family man who needed the job as much as McKenna.

Chapter 31

I, myself, sad to say, once climbed over that fence where Gerry had hung and found the fellow on duty asleep with three heaters around him. Sitting on an armchair, his legs on another, wrapped in a blanket, with a funny, floppy hat on with things covering his ears. It was morning and I couldn't resist hammering on the window. "Patch, I've come to get you," I roared. Heaters, armchairs, blanket, walkie talkie, all went on the floor in a heap.

"What the fuck?" he ran up to the window, stared at me but did not seem to see me.

"What the fuck?"Then he did a very queer thing. He grabbed a baton and ran out the door and off down the yard, as if in pursuit of someone. "What the fuck? What the fuck?"

I was a bit amazed and waited to see what he was going to do next."Patch, come back you gobshite, it's only me, Jimmy."

"What the fuck?" He stopped and seemed to see me for the first time.

"Jimmy."

"Yes, Patch."

"What the fuck?"

"I couldn't agree more, Patch. That says it all."

On duty in the car park one night, towards closing time; it was about 9pm and it closed at 12am. Danny was sober tonight and he and the guard on duty just wanted to go home. Suddenly, a big, drunken, fat man came hurtling down the 'in' ramp, collided with the flimsy wooden barrier which he smashed and fell on his back on the ground.

"Are you alright?"

"Wha' happened? Wha' di hit?"

"You ran into the barrier ol' son."

"Wha' barrier?"

"Never mind, come on and we'll help you up."

"Whes me' car?"

Standing up now and not too apologetic about the smashed barrier but understanding drunks well, and just wanting rid of him, they offered him tea.

"No way!"

So they persuaded him to pay for his exit ticket and sent him down to get his car. Two hours later, still no sign. The guard was dispatched to find him. He found him, lying on his back, out cold; driver's door open with one foot in the car. I think in the end, poor Danny had to drive him home, though how they got him sober enough to give directions was anybody's guess.

Relationships between people are a constant fascination. There was a fellow, an attendant in the car park, who had one of the strangest relationships with his wife I had yet seen. Of course he was an alcoholic. She was too, but not as bad as him. When he was off the drink he would buy her every modern convenience, stereos, videos, TVs, jewellery and so on. Then he would go back on the beer, she would kick him out of the house at a certain point and as times got tight she would sell all the things he had bought her, to feed herself and the children. When he sobered up and she was stuck for money, she would take him back in again and so the cycle would begin again.

Christmas came and the boys were all going drinking after work. A blazing row broke out between McCann and his wife, during which he hit her and knocked her cold. All the lads were going off. So he picked her up and placed her in a shopping trolley and wheeled her away to go drinking with them.

Said he, "I couldn't go drinkin' at Christmas without my Jenny." As far as I know they're still together. You figure it out.

Back in the outside car parks, which were near some really rough tenements, the attendants knew that if they were robbed while on duty the company policy was to pay them a bonus on pay day, for enduring the stress of a robbery. So every long weekend, they were going on the beer, the staff would arrange for one of their friends to don a balaclava and rob them. They all got their bonuses and a small cut from the robbery as well. How clever was that? A good weekend was had by one and all.

Chapter 32

One of our number was on duty at a late night shop in Dublin City Centre. In the City you just never knew what was going to happen. It was where the lunatics in our society seemed to congregate in their greatest number and if you could possibly avoid it, you didn't get involved. Any screwball could have a knife, a broken bottle, a meat cleaver or even a gun, though at that time guns were not as prominent as they are today. Mostly if a 'free for all' erupted involving more than two people, you kept a low profile and called the Gardaí and your mobile supervisor in the van.

A couple of drunks started to punch the heads off each other in front of the shop on the footpath. Our man Larry wisely kept out of it. It was not affecting him or the shop, leave well enough alone. One fellow seemed to be giving the other a right good pasting. One fellow hit the ground. A self righteous middle aged lady approached Larry and told him that he was "a disgrace to his uniform" for not intervening.

"Nothing to do with me missus I only do the shop"

"Well," she said, "I'm going to have to talk to someone about this."

While she was speaking the fellow on the ground, who clearly wasn't as dead as he looked, grabbed her handbag saying something like, "Gimme that bleedin' bag ya snobby oul cow."

His friend had other ideas and in his smelly beer sodden state grabbed her and started to grope her all over.

"Any chance of an oul ride off ya Mrs."

She screeched and struggled to hold onto her handbag and her virtue, such as it was. She started screaming "You filthy animals, you brutes, you savages..."

Larry got the groper off her, long enough for her to wallop the semi prone would be, bag snatcher on the ground encouraging him to release her leg before she bolted down the Main Street in floods of tears, not feeling quite as self righteous as before. The groper called Larry "an arsehole" for intervening. The groper helped bag snatcher up. They said they were friends again, gave each other a big hug with tears in their eyes and staggered off down the street singing with their arms around each other; friends once more.

A couple of nights later in the Car Park down the road Lester, the cash box man was on duty. The car park fellows seemed to think it was their God given right to swindle all and sundry, the bosses, the public, even the coke machine got robbed. In any case Lester and another fellow were on duty. Our Guard was up on the floors checking the cars. Lester got a bit greedy and short changed two cars that went out, in sequence, by a lot. Subsequently one of the cars returned and out stepped a giant, with big Doc Martin boots, and shoulders and arms like a gorilla. He was not a happy giant. "Yez thievin' cunts, I don't mind yez robbin' me but yez robbed me little brother as well. Gimme our money now."

"No problem," said the other attendant. "Sorry about that," as he franticly opened his till to return the man's money, even though it was not he who had taken it.

Lester, who grew up in a rough area was not terribly big, but fancied himself as bit of a "hardman," which he really was not, even though he talked the talk, he could not really walk the walk so to speak.

"What the fuck are you sayin!?" shouted Lester and charged out of the cash box to meet the giant head on.

"Bam!"

One of the giant's big fists caught Lester under the jaw and actually lifted him and sent him flying through the air. He landed in a heap beside the cash box out cold.

"Mister, here's your money," said Danny the other attendant.

"Shove it up your hole," said the giant, so saying, he got in his car and drove away.

A crack in the head can do funny things to a man and Lester was no exception. When he came to, the guard and Danny helped him up but he shrugged them off and promptly fell down again. Finally he found his feet

"I'll teach that fucker I haveta get the rods and the dogs"

And so promptly, he jumped into his car and drove off. Danny and the security guard looked at each other. "What did he say?"

"I haven't a clue, something about rods and dogs, would he be goin' fishin?"

"No ya eejit a rod means a gun, I think"

"Whats he goin'ta shoot?"

"Fucked if I know, your man is probably at home in bed by now!"

"He probably is."

Lester duly arrived back an hour later with two big slobbering Rottweillers in the back of his car and wouldn't you know it, two loaded shotguns in the boot of his car. To the amazement of his comrades and the car park users, he grabbed a loaded gun and with his two big dogs on leads proceeded to be dragged around the car park by the dogs, to what purpose no one rightly knew. But the car park customers must have concluded that the car park company were becoming much more proactive on security and they proceeded with all due haste to the exit asking no questions, but keeping low. The car park cleared early that night; I can't think why. Can you?

Chapter 33

Things have a way of coming around and of course around they came. What do you know, Eddie and Brutus the guard dog wound up alone together on a building site. Brutus was the poor dog who got clobbered by Eddie with the sweeping brush for eating his sandwiches. So it was that I came on duty one evening to find the compound gate locked and no security guard ready and eager to go home. It was Saturday evening, a rare night to be off, much sought after by us as an opportunity for a real night "on the town" at the weekend. So I was indeed surprised not to be greeted as usual by the guard at the gate with a hasty, "Right here's the keys good luck, I'm off." A disappearing act worthy of Houdini himself.

I called at first, no reply. Then I heard the dog barking and growling and snapping. So I went around outside the fence until I came on the scene of the action.

Here was Brutus under a tree snapping and jumping as high as he could, to get at Eddie who was roaring down at it, "Go way you psycho bastard dog. Let me down."

"Evenin' Eddie. How's things? Playin with the doggie are we?."

"Stop messin' about Jimmy, I'm stuck up here the last four hours. Lucky I was near a tree. Look, look what he did to me."

He showed me his behind, his bare behind. Brutus had seized the backside of his trousers as he scurried up into the tree and left sizeable teeth marks on his buttocks.

"Begod Eddie you have an awful hairy arse."

"Jimmy I'm not fuckin' laughin' help me will ya'. I've a bleedin' date tonight. I'm not goin' to spend it here."

"What did I tell you about hittin' guard dogs Eddie. I told ya you'd be sorry."

"Alright, alright Jimmy ya' told me so, you were right all along. Are ya' happy now, please Jimmy."

It was an eight foot high fence with spikes on top and it took some doing on my part to get in but eventually I did; retrieved the dog and locked him in a shed so that Eddie could get down and leave the site alive.

"So what on earth happened?"

"I was goin' on a patrol, the dog was tryin' to get at me all through the shift and I threw a stone at him and told him to shut up, Next thing he bites through the lead tyin' him to the pole and comes after me like the psycho dog that he is. I knew I was dead if he got me, so I ran for the tree as fast as I could. I jumped for that high branch but before I could get up properly the dog got me by the arse and nearly pulled me out of the tree. Lucky the trousers ripped and I managed to escape. How am I goin' ta' get the bus home like this Jimmy?" Once more he showed me his arse.

We found a pair of tatty overalls belonging to the workers and I loaned him my anorak and after a cup of tea to steady his nerves and brief examination of his posterior to ensure that he had stopped bleeding. I raided the First Aid Kit, threw some disinfectant on it before I sent him on his way.

"Ya' needn't be telling the lads I was slappin' bandages on your hairy arse."

"You can be damn sure I won't and you don't say it either. That Fagan fella is a bit of a bumboy, he might want to have a look at it himself."

"He probably would." We both laughed.

"Jimmy...thanks, have a good night."

"I will. Go out get twisted and be sure and give that young wan' you're meetin' a good rattle tonight."

"You can count on that, see ya' Jimmy." So saying, he ran for the bus he could see coming down the hill. I retrieved Brutus from the shed and we went for a patrol. "Brutus," I said, "I think you have been a naughty boy."

He wagged his tail and licked my hand.

Chapter 34

Time had passed, I was now a married man with my young wife expecting our first baby. Her time was near. I was back on duty in the quarry. I had one of the early mobile phones which weighed quite a bit with me on standby for when the call came. There were three others on duty also in different parts of the complex, the block factory, the main gate and the offices. I was at the back gate and my area also included the quarry itself, which was about a mile wide and about 300 feet (about 100 metres) deep; it was big and scary and dark. It was lashing rain that night and going up and down to the quarry was tricky enough at the best of times but when it rained like this, it was a nightmare.

We had to check a pump at the base of the quarry every two hours. If it shut down we had to immediately restart it, otherwise the whole quarry would flood and access to the electrics would be under water and it might be weeks before production could resume and I might be looking for a new job.

So I went down yet again but as I came down the slope I slipped and fell on my arse, lost my mobile phone in the blackness and also my torch and radio.

"Shit, shit, where are you?" I fumbled around in the darkness and the rough ground trying to find them. I was about fifteen minutes searching when the radio crackled to life; one of the lads was doing a radio check. I quickly stumbled towards the sound and found the radio and sure enough the torch was beside it. I then used the torch to find the mobile phone. Everything was wet but still working. The rain was pelting now. I quickly checked the pump, clocked the key and noted the time in my notebook and went back up, had a cup of tea and dried myself off by the heater.

As I came down for my next check I heard a big rumble and a crash.

I shone my torch as I went; when I got to the place I had fallen earlier the whole place was strewn with heavy rocks and boulders of every size. Some fell with such force they were embedded into the ground as if shot from a gun. They had landed exactly where I had been looking for my phone, torch, and radio. The rain was eroding the walls of the quarry and causing boulders and rocks to come crashing down in the darkness. Had it happened a bit earlier I might have become a permanent fixture in the quarry, buried into the ground by those lethal rocks. I quickly checked the pump and ran back up to the safety of the hut and vowed not to go down again until daylight.

I put my head on my arm on the desk, to doze a while. It seemed I had scarcely slept when my mobile rang. "I think it's startin', she wailed. "Me waters have broken, I'm scared, will ya' hurry and come home."

"Yes, yes alright, don't panic, don't panic, keep calm and don't panic...ah okay, okay let's see what'll I do now," still groggy waking up fast.

"Come home quick," she wailed, "The waters have gone all over the floor, help me will ya!"

"Yes, yes I will, don't panic, keep calm, keep calm I better come home then."

"Will ya bloody well hurry up."

"Okay, okay, right, right, yes, yes, I'm on my way dear."

Eventually I got my head together and radioed for one of the lads to come down to relieve me so I could go. The site leading patrolman came down himself, "Off ya' go Jimmy good luck, if it's a boy name it after me."

"You must be joking I might ruin him for life."

He laughed and raised the barrier to let me drive out. Now I had a car also. I shot out the gate like a greyhound out of a trap in a big race and I drove like a madman on wet roads in a kind of daze. It was a wonder I made it home alive at all but someone was on my side that night and I got only green lights on my way and very little traffic. A lucky thing with the maniac way I was driving.

When I got to the house she was ready at the door with her bag packed. "Get me to the hospital and try not to kill the two of us."
"Yes, yes, right, right, yes, yes….."
"Shut up gibbering and get into the car will you."
"Ah yes, yes…."
I drove not much better to the hospital as she would give an occasional loud screech which would nearly send me off the road, interspersed with, "Mind that car, watch out for that old lady… those lights were red… ya'll kill the two of us."
"Yes, yes."
We got there alive, then the nurses took over, thank God.
"Jim don't leave me," she wailed.
"Okay, okay, I'm coming dear."
"Shut up with your dear, I have a first name haven't I"?
"Yes, yes."
And so it was our first born child was a little dark haired baby girl and we named her Stephanie.

Of course after the baby was born our world changed drastically. Neither I nor my wife got much sleep. We were living in a rough neighbourhood in the South City. The house was always cold no matter what we did. I would come home in the morning after working a long night shift and try to get some sleep. She would be exhausted having had to get up a number of times during the night, to attend to the baby. I remember collapsing into bed one morning and my wife said "Here hold her while I get dressed."

I duly complied and I lifted my little daughter high in the air as I lay in bed and said "Now how is my pretty, little girl this morning?"

She replied with a loud burp and promptly threw up all over me, saturating the bed and coating my face and glasses. She then started to bawl her head off. Ah! The joys of parenthood! Some time later, after changing the bed and washing the sick off myself, I eventually did get back to bed and some sleep. My poor wife was struggling also: a first baby can really take you by storm. Because the house was always cold, the only way we could be sure she would be warm enough at night was to take her into the bed with us and try not to roll over on top of the little body in our sleep. She for her part, would poo, wee, throw up, scream her head off and generally kept us on our toes. While many people in the neighbourhood were decent, hard working people, there were enough of thugs and ruffians to make life eventful. My next door neighbour and I each had a brick put through our front windows on separate occasions, not the same brick you understand. Cars were set alight. Stolen cars were driven up and down the street at high speed in hopes of attracting the Gardaí into giving them a chase, their idea of fun.

I was on duty in a factory in North Dublin one night. A quiet, tedious, night. At 5 a.m. my wife rang me on my mobile phone. The baby was screaming in the background, augmented by what sounded like a fireworks display going on outside, punctuated by shrill police or fire brigade sirens. "What's going on ? Are you alright?"I said.

"This shithole! They're burnin' cars or vans or somethin', it's like a bloody warzone here" she wailed into the telephone. "Even our poor dogs in the back yard are tryin' ta' hide from the noise."

Apparently as I found out the next day, some bright spark, on his way home from the pub, thought it would be a bit of fun to set fire to a large van parked across the road from our house. He broke a window and threw a flaming, petrol soaked rag into it and up it went. When its brake lines burned through, it duly rolled backwards down the hill, smacked into a parked car and drove it into four more cars and up went the lot. If it weren't for the fire brigade it would probably have burned down a nearby block of flats as well. There were exploding petrol tanks and engines, black smoke everywhere; a madhouse. This was what woke up my wife and baby. "Can ya' come home I'm scared," she pleaded.

By the time I had calmed her down on the phone, it was daylight and all was quiet. So I said I might as well finish the shift and come home. That morning I decided, if it killed me I would get us another house. It certainly took some doing but eventually I did just that.

We were still struggling with not much sleep and even less money, but we were young and we soldiered on.

Chapter 35

A guard was on duty at a certain Bank; a courier arrived and gave him a package with allegedly £10,000 therein. When the package was handed in, it was slightly empty, in fact, completely empty. Accusations flew. The courier said it was the guard, the guard said it was the courier, but nobody knew for sure. We never found out. From that day on Robbie became known as the £10,000 man.

The manager of the car park was having staff problems. One fellow had got into a huff and went over to the pub. The manager waited an hour and sent over another fellow to get him but he also forgot to come back, so, foolishly he sent over another fellow and guess what, no sign of him either. Eventually he went over himself, leaving the security guard in charge, thinking his sizeable frame, coming through the door, would scare them into line. When he got there, all three were sitting at the counter, drinking away. He was about to speak when the first offender spoke up.

"Listen, fat boy, either sit down and have a drink with us or fuck off."

He meekly sat down, had a drink with them and finally coaxed them all back to the car park an hour later.

A new fellow had started with us.He said to me, "People will have to respect my authority while I'm in uniform."

"Ah no," I thought. "Not another fool."

Aloud I said, "Good for you."

He had found a six year old boy playing at the bottom of the car park with a friend, so he produced a pair of handcuffs, real ones, and handcuffed the little boy's hands behind his back and marched him up to the cash box. The little boy's friend told the boy's mother who had nipped across to the shop before going home. Meantime, the little boy howled. She returned with a real policeman in tow who said if he didn't immediately remove those cuffs he could find himself wearing a pair too. I'm glad to say he didn't last too long after that.

Another new boy got cold while minding an office block, so he decided to gather some paper and timber to light a nice little fire to warm himself; in the office, on the floor, in the middle of a really expensive deep pile carpet. When the fire got going, he realised the carpet was on fire. He stomped out the fire and then saw the huge hole in the carpet, so he panicked and ran out, leaving the keys in the door and the door unlocked and that was how Benny found it with the carpet still smouldering. We never saw him again either.

It's hard to remember everything that happened. Some events I find hard to believe myself. Some were so complicated and crazy it would actually be hard to get them onto paper. The years passed, we all got older, some died, some had families, some got married, others divorced, some changed jobs, mostly we lost touch and went our separate ways. I can't say that I loved the job, but it was a living. There were many shopping centres and buildings which would not exist now, had people like us not stayed up all night to mind them and worked at Christmas and weekends when others slept or socialised.

It was a thankless, boring, tedious job, with long, unsociable hours and bad pay. There were many I knew who would gain far more from the work we did, than we ever would, and never lose a wink of sleep in the process, whether it was our bosses or the owners of the businesses we guarded. I think the only redeeming features of the job were the characters we met and the crazy events like those recorded here. I recall many cold, dismal, lonely nights, walking around in all weathers, missing my nice, warm bed, doing sixteen and twenty-four hour shifts on occasion, always tired, often miserable. I see young fellows now taking the job so seriously and I want to be sick. Few lasted very long who had not got that one crucial ingredient: a sense of humour. I'm a bit like the fellow when his grandson asked him what he did in World War II. He replied "I did one very important thing."

"Oh! And what was that?" said the little boy, all eager.

"I survived it."

That about sums up my own attitude to security work and the years I put in.

The Life and Times of a 'Gotcha'

For further copies of this book please contact:

Email:
Jameslinn48@Gmail.com

Or write to:
James Linnane,
Tattyreagh,
Bailieboro,
County Cavan.
Ireland.

About James Linnane:

James was born on a farm in Galway in 1962, the youngest of a family of ten. His father was a foreman in construction working for the Galway county council as well as being a farmer, although James's mother did much of the running of the farm for many years, as well as raising the children, ("a woman of steel"). Before James was sixteen his family had moved home twice. initially to a farm in Meath and when he was fifteen, to Dublin.

His career covered the bar trade, construction, security work and shop work. He was a bar manager and a builder at different times in his life. He also worked in America for a short time. His first book *Never Take an Irishman Seriously Unless he's Armed* was published in New York in 1988, sadly no longer in print. He has been writing since his late teens. His hobbies have included soccer and Kenpo Karate (he fought in a number of competitions).

He attended a number of schools, in different counties and completed his secondary education in C.B.S. Westland Row in Dublin. He also attended the College of Marketing and Design in later years. He met and married his wife, Karen, in Dublin in the 90's. They have lived in a number of different counties over the years. He is currently a member of both "The Boyne Writers Group" and "The Meath Writers Group" both based in Trim county Meath and proud to be so.

He now resides in Ballivor county Meath with his wife Karen and their two daughters Amber and Stephanie.

$L208,7781$

LEABHARLANN CHONTAE LONGFOIRT

Longford County Library & Arts Services

$920/LIT$

This book should be returned on or before the latest date shown below. Fines on overdue books will accrue on a weekly basis or part thereof.